FREEDOM
TRIUMPHANT
IN
WAR AND PEACE

Ten Commandments:
Today, Yesterday, and Tomorrow

Manuel Antonio Pérez

First Edition   July 2017
Editor in Chief   Jessica M. Pérez
Editor   Christina Cutting
Copy Editor   MrProofReading
Proof Reading   Rubicelia Pérez
Cover Design   Angie Alaya

Imprenta Pérez Familiar
PO Box 2
Spangle, WA 99031

Scripture quotations used in the book are from the following sources:

Scripture taken from the New Century Version®. Copyright © 2005 by Thomas Nelson. Used by permission. All rights reserved.

Scripture quotations marked (NRSV) are taken from the New Revised Standard Version Bible, copyright © 1989 the Division of Christian Education of the National Council of the Churches of Christ in the United States of America. Used by permission. All rights reserved.

Scripture quotations marked (NLT) are taken from the Holy Bible, New Living Translation, copyright © 1996, 2004, 2007 by Tyndale House Foundation. Used by permission of Tyndale House Publishers, Inc., Carol Stream, Illinois 60188. All rights reserved.

Scripture quotations marked (KJV) are taken from The Authorized King James Version of the Bible.

ISBN 978-0-9997135-0-1

I

II

III

HOIVOR

V

VI

VII

VIII

IX

X.

DEDICATION

For my Best Friend and Father, Jehovah.
For my best friend and wife, Jessica.
For my beautiful parents, Dolores and Manuel.
Para mi Familia.
For my boys:
May you live your lives with integrity.
May the truth always set you free.
May you always protect the innocent and weak.
May we someday serve as priests in the realms of eternity.

To those who are locked up and often forgotten,
I remember you.

¹⁴ If my people, which are called by my name,
shall humble themselves, and pray, and seek my face, and turn
from their wicked ways; then will I hear from heaven, and
will forgive their sin, and will heal their land.
2 Chronicles 7:14 KJV

CONTENTS

PREFACE

Last night I had a dream. A group of friends and I were out in the mission field. I cannot say for certain where we were, but we were not in the USA. We were definitely abroad in some kind of subtropical climate; it was somewhat dry in the lowland areas and tropical as we ascended in elevation. We were steadily climbing a rough mountain path, trying to reach what I can only guess would be a village. It was to be our final destination. Here, we met what seemed to be an indigenous group of people. Try as I might, I could not make out their actual cultural heritage, but they resembled an ancient aboriginal people. During the next few clips of memory, we were interacting with the tribe in various activities. At times, we were seen sharing the Good News, and at other times, preoccupied with mundane everyday chores and routine duties. I am not certain how long this lasted, for dreams do not adhere to our conscious rules of time. Fast forward, I remember we were being forced to flee.

For whatever reason, we were led to escape through a treacherous mountain passage. The only sense of direction we had was to travel towards, who I would like to call, the village shaman or medicine man. Once we reached his humble hut, it was obvious he had been expecting us, and he immediately signaled to us that he would be guiding us a short way. He was adamant about trying to communicate to us that we needed to be aware of the snakes. From his gestures and pointing towards his snake-laden shanty, we understood our most pressing danger: Beware of the snake.

We all formed a line behind the medicine man. I was in

the lead, and my friends were following. At a certain point in our descent from the mountain, he, the shaman, would go no further. Instead, he handed me his walking stick and pointed us in the direction we should travel. He used simple gestures to signal to me that I needed to watch (by pointing at his eyes) for snakes (by wriggling his arms and hands). He did so, multiple times, with fervor and panic in his eyes. At this point, we were all filled with a certain amount of fear. I can remember my mates making comments, though I could not make them out because I was lost in my own head, processing the moment and dealing with my own fears.

Hesitantly, we walked down the mountain with focus and attentiveness to our surroundings. "If any of you even see a snake, please let us all know immediately," I said. As we came off the treacherous mountain and into what we most certainly thought was liberation, the clearing at the foot of the mountain, I instantaneously felt fear. I knew we had just walked into the danger zone.

Almost immediately, snakes appeared out of nowhere. Anxiety and panic began to try to overwhelm us, and all I could do was remind everyone to follow in my exact footsteps. The interesting part was that I could see the snakes in my mind, but I was blind to them in my path. "Do not be afraid. I can feel the snakes. I know where they are, so just follow me, and we will get out of this," I reassuringly told the others.

I can recall having watched the old medicine man and his every step along the way. I remembered how he moved and when he did so. I especially was reminded of how he moved his staff. I began to move the same. We moved in rhythm and syncopation, almost as if in a choreographed dance—something that resembled the art of Tai Chi but with constant forward movement and with the staff to lean upon. We moved steadily forward, stepping over and around snakes that I could only see in my mind. My companions were scared and could see each and every one of the snakes, plain as day. Somehow, I had become blind, so I had to depend on my "mind's eye" to guide me through the snakes and lead my best friends out of there.

As we approached a clearing, I can remember feeling a sense of calm, so we continued to walk forward. Right away, as the sun began to shine, we felt that fear again. There were snakes in the vicinity, only this time, no one could see them. What I experienced next was the interesting part; it seemed as though the snakes were appearing out of nowhere. Immediately, I began to wave the staff above the ground from left to right in an attempt to expose the snakes, while startling them out from in front of our path. My friends were skeptical of this approach; nevertheless, I reassured them that they had to believe. Eventually, with this method, we approached what seemed to be a village, and flowers appeared on the ground in front of where I was diligently and repeatedly waving the staff.

Upon awakening, I knew this dream had a special significance. You see, I had been praying lately for a method as to how I should begin to write this book. I am not a theologian. I do, however, have a significant amount of life experience and have experienced many things that most of you never have and most likely never will. Believe me when I say that you should count your blessings.

I have concluded that the old medicine man in my dream was Life. Life experience is what called us in the appropriate direction, and it was life experience that would guide us from harm. However, life experience could only take us so far. The only thing life was certain of was the dangers that lie ahead, particularly those of a cunning nature. The snakes, well, I am certain you can deduce what or who those might have been in reference to, i.e., various sins and temptations. The most interesting part, however, was the staff. You may have already gathered this, but the walking stick, or staff, I believe represented the Bible. At a certain point in every person's life, we must make a choice to venture into the unknown, especially amongst a scary and severely unpredictable journey with certain danger and possible death around the corner. The old wise medicine man understood that the only thing that would get us through was by walking as he did, with the staff right out in front of him, one step at a time.

It was no accident that the staff was handed to me. It may be that I have more "life experience" than the others. It may simply mean we should all follow suit. More importantly, however, during my training as a disciple of Christ, I have always felt that the Bible and the Bible alone should be our ultimate guide while attempting to navigate this life. Human error is far too great when measured against a realm of eternal and infinite significance. Many scholars have argued there is far too much human error in the Bible to make it accurate. However, they fail by missing the point, I believe. The fact that this one Book, with its multiple authors, and written during various times in Earth's history, somehow accurately points to the cross and breathes testimony as to who Jesus really is—Supreme Ruler of the universe.

So, what I attempt to do here is simple. I use life experience, good or bad, to justify the validity of God's Sovereign Law. It is my hope that, in painting an accurate picture of these laws, not as restrictions but as liberation, you will find inspiration and search for God with all your heart.

It has been said that, in modern life, there is nothing certain other than death and taxes. There is one other assurance that trumps each of those and will continue to do so for eternity. It is certain that Jesus is the Way, the Truth, and the Life...a declaration that is relevant in the grand scheme of time, space, and existence. In the blink of an eye, all of life will be lost, except for those who love Him and keep His commandments. Obedience, as an act of love and respect, in our short time on this earth is a small price to pay for an immortal life as kings and queens as recompense.

Faith always sees best in the dark.

ACKNOWLEDGEMENTS

Where would I be without the support of my wife? Words can't express the amount of gratitude I have, not only for your help on this project, but your unwavering support in all of my dreams and aspirations. This book truly would not have come to fruition had it not been for your professional, academic, and most importantly, spiritual insight. Your unique perspective guided by your own intimate relationship with Christ, coupled with your delicate sense of compassion and empathy towards our fellow man, have provided valuable direction at many points along this journey. Not to mention the times you held me up when I was weak, and helped me up when I fell. For you, I am eternally grateful, My Love.

Manuel and Dolores Pérez: Our journey has been an interesting one. It has certainly been a story of redemption and salvation and one that continues to impact many lives across multiple communities. Above all things, we have been given the opportunity to grow together as children in the sight of God and beneath his watchful care. My life experience and the richness that I now endure is a direct result of your willingness to love me, each in your individual ways. Mom, you are the portrait of Christ that I aspire to be, and I measure every human I have ever encountered against your Sainthood. If I could describe you in one word, it would surely be: Love. Apa, we have had a unique, often turbulent, and interesting relationship, to say the least. At this point in my life, as wisdom becomes my default method of judging all things, I have learned that you are a champion in this thing we call life, and it has been my privilege to learn invaluable spoken and unspoken lessons from you. Together, we move forward as elders into eternity and that anticipated banquet table at the feet of the Almighty. Someday, I will compose a volume in which the world will know how great your sacrifices were for our (your children's) success and how true it is that "the family that prays together, succeeds together."

Pastor Ron, you, my friend, were catapulted into my life at a time when I was certainly at cross-roads. Life has definitely not been kind to me on many occasions, some of which was my fault, and some of which, well, such is life. I am certain the Spirit certainly led me to the tent that fateful day, and as a result, I was introduced to a man who would ultimately help to guide me back to the place where I really belonged, back home into the Kingdom of Heaven. Thank you for being my mentor, and to this day, my ordination as an elder under your watchful care is one of my crowning achievements in life, and I revere it dearly. Thank you for your contributions to this work, and for your guidance. I am certain that we have been chosen to battle against the enemy side by side until the final day. It is and always shall be an honor to be your servant.

To all of those who made this book possible, I will never forget you and your kindness. Blessings will fall upon you because of your decision to commit to this project. Thank you.

And before I go, Father, you know all things. You know that my heart is heavy as I write to you now. This world is need of your light, your mercy, your peace, truth, and your unconditional love. It still blows my mind that it has already been freely given. You have set me free from many chains of bondage, much pain, and a life filled with regrets. And now I enjoy a life with my eyes wide open, my heart filled with joy and peace, and eagerness to share true hope with my neighbors. Thank you for choosing me to write this book. Thank you for collaborating with me on this project. I am your servant now and forever, and I praise you with my life. To You be the kingdom, the power, and the glory forever. Amen

Freedom Triumphant in War and Peace

PARTE

UNO

³⁶ "Teacher, which command in the
law is the most important?"
³⁹ And the second command is like the first:
'Love your neighbor as you love yourself.'
New Century Version (NCV)

³⁶ "Teacher, which commandment in the law is the greatest?"
³⁹ And a second is like it: 'You shall love
your neighbor as yourself.'
New Revised Standard Version (NRSV)

³⁶ Master, which is the great commandment in the law?
³⁹ And the second is like unto it, Thou
shalt love thy neighbour as thyself.
The Authorized King James Version (KJV)

Matthew 22:36, 39

PROLOGUE

CONCERNING HUMANITY

Crimes against humanity are committed daily. You might be thinking that is such a vague statement, such an umbrella phrase that sounds like the introduction to some kind of political rant. Well, to be completely honest, it somewhat is. We all know what crime is, but what is humanity?

The greatest crime ever perpetrated upon citizens of our earth is the proposed notion that one human is less than another. This is one of the greatest lies ever told. As a result of such an insane ideology, countless individuals have been beaten, mutilated, humiliated, driven to insanity, and murdered in cold blood simply because they did not fit an accepted belief construct. The greatest question one should ask his/herself is, "How it is possible for humans to be so cruel to other humans?"

As creatures of highest intelligence and beings with the ability to reason, it should be derived that we might see beyond the veils of our physical differences within our species and search deep within the souls of each other to recognize that we are all essentially the same. No one above the other, no one beneath, an equal distribution of talents and skills, knowledge, and ability across the board from person to person, regardless of ethnic origins.

So, I ask again, what is humanity? The human race is a privileged kingdom. Creatures above all others created in the likeness of Gods. And yet, we act out and treat our fellow man worse than rabid beasts. What on earth has forced us to become so very inhumane? Why would you treat your neighbor with less care and compassion than a dog or a cat left for dead in the street? Why do we reject our neighbors?

I have to say the answer to that question lies in the same answer Christ Himself proposed to those who tried to trap Him. It is precisely because we love ourselves that we have forgotten our humanity. Let me point out, however, love and compassion are not the same. Humans are selfish creatures. The will to survive, and the instincts instilled within us for survival have one absolute objective, and that objective is to preserve our own lives at any time we are threatened and at whatever the cost. The problem herein is that we have created perceived threats where no threat actually exists. The truth is that past experiences and oftentimes trauma have cultivated our current patterns of thought. Our perceptions are the true culprits. It is these patterns of thought that ultimately determine our action or inaction within any supposed survival context. Consequentially, it is the fear of the unknown that has prompted us to categorize the unknown as a threat, rather than approach it with casual curiosity and wonder. People who are different than we are in a myriad of ways are automatically placed in the "caution" bin, rather than being allowed to express their inner shine and showcase their individuality. Remember, we were ALL created in the likeness of God.

Clearly, nothing in life is black or white, which is my point. It has been said that most of life happens in the beauty found within the gray, the proverbial meshing of various colors, hues, tints, and patterns. It is evident now, more than ever, beauty is found at every corner and within every hidden knoll. The inevitable proliferation of modernization, interconnection, globalization, and electronic social gatherings have helped to alleviate many of the aforementioned pressures and the anxiety of voyaging into the unknown. Because of the expanse of technology, we as a people have begun to understand for the first time in history that, as a species, we humans are in the exact same struggle alongside every other species.

Our planet and its nature, all things great and small, everything that is part of the great circle of life exists in harmony with our humanity. Only unity can sustain its beauty; only vanity can destroy its existence. Who is my neighbor? Look to your left, and look to your right. Turn your eyes above and then below and see who is by your side. That person standing there beside you is your neighbor and your potential friend. Yes, I know, the enemy lurks ever closer. I ask you once more, who is your neighbor?

The command to love your neighbor in the same way you love yourself is as simple as it reads. If you love yourself with a selfish looking-out-for-number-one type of love, then your perspective towards your fellow man will be found to be severely lacking. But if you are good to yourself, recognizing your faults and accepting your mistakes, striving to be the best version of you and exercising true unadulterated love and compassion towards yourself, then your actions and desires for others will mirror the same internal motives for their betterment. Do you value your own life? Do you know your true worth? "For God so loved the world, that He gave His only begotten Son, that whosoever believeth in Him, should have eternal life." (John 3:16).

Human life is so precious and so priceless that God descended onto the face of the earth. He took on human form to walk among His creation and fully understand the complexity of the human condition, only to be beaten, mutilated, humiliated, driven towards severe mental distress, and executed in cold blood, so that you might live life in abundance. Allow me to answer the question for you then. Your neighbor is every person born into this world and conceived as part of this life. The blood of the innocent God-man, Christ, flows within the hearts and veins of every human being, and just as the color is the same scarlet hue in every mortal, so we also are connected. A royal race, the human race, a nation where God is Supreme Father, and we are all brothers and sisters. And so, we are challenged with loving our brother and sister as we love ourselves.

The process of self-examination is vital in understanding the root of one's actions or reactions. "What is causing the quarrels and fights among you? Don't they come from the evil desires at war within you? You want what you don't have, so you scheme and kill to get it. You are jealous of what others have, but you can't get it, so you fight and wage war to take it away from them. Yet you don't have what you want because you don't ask God for it. And even when you ask, you don't get it because your motives are all wrong—you want only what will give you pleasure." (James 4:1-3 NLT) At the end of the day, if you have no love or respect for yourself, then it will be extremely difficult for you to have any type of true and lasting love for your neighbor because your motives are all wrong.

Self-love is important. It is a necessary component for the ultimate human experience. Self-absorption and alienation, on the other hand, are dangerous and destructive. Therefore, by subscribing to these commands, you are inadvertently showing love to yourself and to others and demonstrating supreme respect towards all things that are important to humans in each human experience, and ultimately, to God Himself.

X

¹⁷ "You must not want to take your neighbor's house. You must not want his wife or his male or female slaves, or his ox or his donkey, or anything that belongs to your neighbor." NCV

¹⁷ You shall not covet your neighbor's house; you shall not covet your neighbor's wife, or male or female slave, or ox, or donkey, or anything that belongs to your neighbor. NRSV

¹⁷ Thou shalt not covet thy neighbour's house, thou shalt not covet thy neighbour's wife, nor his manservant, nor his maidservant, nor his ox, nor his ass, nor any thing that is thy neighbour's. KJV

Exodus 20:17

CHAPTER ONE

THE 10TH COMMANDMENT

America the Great, America the Beautiful! America, the one place on the face of the earth where you can be what you want to be, do what you want to do (within the confines of the law of course), live where you want to live, and have what you want to have. The possibilities truly are endless. Some of you reading this may just shrug at the profundity of the previous statements. Others of you, especially those who have had an opportunity to visit another country (specifically a third world country), have true appreciation for those few facts that I just lined out.

Now, I come from a poor family. I mean poor for American standards—as in, we lived most of our lives below the poverty line. My perspective on the word "poor," however, has changed in my adulthood, and I will dive into that here in a few minutes. But for us growing up, we had a tiny one-bedroom home, old clunker cars, hand-me-down clothes, yard sale toys, stood in line for government cheese, so on and so forth, you get the picture.

This situation left a lot of room for desire.

As a child, it was easy to want something so very badly. To put it on countless birthday wish-lists, Christmas wish-lists, to wish upon the rare falling star only to have those dreams never come true, for them never to become a reality. Or there was also the oftentimes immediate dream crushing ability of Mom, who would shut us down dead in our tracks before the eyes would get all cute and the bottom lip began to quiver. Nope! Mom wasn't having any of that today. We would then have to turn around, hold on dearly to the desired package, and walk back to the toy aisle, returning it to the shelf. Once it was back up there, we would proceed to walk to and fro in the aisle and keep an eye on it while other children came in and out of the perpetual trap, better known as the toy aisle. I would like to note that I had a trick, though. I would stash my desired toy in a secret spot, oftentimes in a location way far away from the original location, in hopes that, someday, when I would return, my toy of choice would still be there. I don't think that trick ever worked out for me; however, psychologically you see, psychologically I would always be victorious, even though Mom had just laid the smackdown.

Of course, as fate would have it, the next time you go over to a friend's house, they have that very toy, the very model you cried yourself to sleep about, just lying there on the floor. The toy is dirty; sometimes just dust from sitting around but other times caked with mud and rejected, set aside to be forgotten in the sea of other toys in the friend's palace of a bedroom. In your mind, you immediately ask them "Why?! Why would you mistreat such a treasure?" and at that very instant, you begin to feel ill. Sick with the thought of, "If I had only been born rich like so and so, I would *never* treat my toys like this..."

I cannot tell you the countless times this happened. That desire, that urge to have what was not mine creeping into my mind and almost immediately creeping into my soul and soon after becoming an obsession. Would my friend even notice that it was gone? What if I just borrowed it for a few days? I would only be borrowing it to clean it up for him/her, after all. Yes, I must confess that I, as perfect as I may be now, was tempted by the desire for my friend's toys at times. Fortunately enough, though, I grew up, and those kinds of desires have never leaped into my mind again.

When I was younger still, I read God's rule, His commandment: "You shall not covet your neighbor's house;

you shall not covet your neighbor's wife, or male or female slave, or ox, or donkey, or anything that belongs to your neighbor" (Exodus 20:17 NRSV). First, the only words I understood in that entire first part of the sentence were neighbor and house, and since I had absolutely NO idea whatsoever what the word covet could possibly mean, I immediately thought it was something that only adults do. You know, since covet is clearly an adult word and therefore had no relevance to me since I was just a little guy. Then the verse talks about my neighbor's wife, clearly not meant for children. The neighbor's male servants and female servants? This was clearly not written for people in my time. Nobody even knows what an ox is; I know what a donkey is, and what exactly does "*anything*" really mean?

It should be clear to us all now that number 10 was not intended for anyone younger than those of legal age to work in your particular state of residence. This was definitely one that was intended for adults and adults only. After all, I am just a kid, and I really only understand the example my adults are handing down to me, right?

Herein lies a huge problem. Growing up is sometimes such a painstaking process. Long gone are the days when our biggest worry was what we would be having for lunch or dinner on any particular day. I know that, even in America today, there are some who still have food as their main concern, but for the most part, when one becomes an adult, life becomes a little bit more complex. Sadly enough, if a person is an adult in this country and finds themselves wanting for their next meal, it is most likely due to an inferior situation that led them to be where they are.

So, what does it mean for adults? What does it mean when it says, "You should not want to take your neighbor's house?" What exactly is being said here? As a carpenter, I have been privileged to build many houses in my lifetime. I can say one thing for certain. The act of physically taking your neighbor's house is most certainly not what this verse is referring to. If we take it back to the old-school word "covet," I think it is much easier to understand. Good old Merriam-Webster says that to covet means to "wish for earnestly" or "to desire." There is that word again, desire. But what could possibly be wrong with desiring your neighbor's house? After all, we are all in pursuit of the big American Dream, are we not? So if my neighbor has a pretty nice, big, McMansion of a house, then why can't I have what he has?

In the pursuit of happiness, I honestly don't think there is anything wrong with wanting nice things. Now, I am speaking in an American context, because I have been blessed with the privilege of being born into this great nation and all its endless possibilities. However, this verse is not directed only towards Americans. It is directed at all the citizens of this world. I believe this verse has an underlying tone or meaning that leans towards "obsession." Yes, the word is "covet" or "desire," although I believe it actually means to desire for *obsessively*. Now here folks, here is where we can run into a lot of problems.

"Obsession" by simple definition, according to good ol' Merriam Webster, is such:

- "a state in which someone thinks about someone or something constantly or frequently especially in a way that is not normal"
- "someone or something that a person thinks about constantly or frequently"
- "an activity that someone is very interested in or spends a lot of time doing"

There is nothing wrong with wanting a house like your neighbor's. He or she has probably worked extremely hard for it. Or maybe they came into it through someone else's hard work. It doesn't matter. Either way, there is essentially nothing wrong with wanting a nice house, even if you want it to be like your neighbor's. However, the moment you have to have your house *exactly* like your neighbor's house, you are going to have problems. It is not going to be good for anyone if it so happens that you decide you have to paint your house the same matching colors as your neighbor's. Or you decide to put up a cute little white fence just because your neighbor did. Or you plant the same exact flowers in front of your house. Maybe even go so far as to uproot some tree from somewhere just to have it transplanted in your front yard to match the neighbor's maple tree with a tire swing in it. Same tire. Same swing blowing in the wind. No! That is creepy! Not to mention exhausting for you! Let me suggest something to you. It is much more exhausting to try to copy someone or something than it is to be original. The reason is because originality is natural. When YOU are YOU, then all you have to do is identify and apply. When you decide you want to copycat, then you have to research before you can implement or apply. Believe me when I tell you, research is the part that can be brutal.

Are you still not convinced? How are you going to go over to the neighbor's house and chip off some of their paint so you can match it perfectly? How are you going to be snapping pictures of every flower and trying to buy the exact same ones? How are you going to get a tree with the exact same branches to hang the tire swing from? That noise is just exhausting! Just stop it already.

We haven't even touched the fact that your obsession is going to bring out some weird and extremely noticeable behaviors in you. What happens when your neighbor buys a new car? You can't afford a new BMW, or a motorcycle, and you don't even know how to ride! Or a cat? You are allergic to cats. What if the neighbor decides to buy a pony? What in the world are you going to do with a pony? You have never even ridden a horse in your life! I know I am jumping the gun a little bit and skipping forward to the *"or anything that is your neighbor's"* part, but I couldn't help myself.

The Neighbor's Wife

So, now that we have the creepy obsession with the neighbor's house out of the way, let's talk about his wife. I am going to touch more on this subject a little later in this book because this topic is so critical that there is a sovereign rule against following through with your obsessive desire for your neighbor's wife and making the terrible mistake of making her your own. This is a can of worms that most people have never imagined would ever ruin their lives.

Now, for the sake of illustration, I am going to be gender specific here. I am going to relate to the coveting of the neighbor's wife; however, this information can surely be applied to coveting the neighbor's husband as well. You know, the fireman next door? I am a man, so I will be referring to wife and not the hunky neighborhood firefighter. What about desiring your neighbor's wife is wrong? After all, she is probably beautiful, sexy, funny, and intelligent, and she always looks so perfectly made up, am I right? She works out all the time and is always ready to be so helpful. One cannot help but desire her.

First things first, please understand the neighbor's wife belongs to the neighbor, not as a possession, except by promise. This happens to be a mutual promise and agreement that is actually recognized by modern law. That should mean to you that she is off-limits, both within the realms of morality and within the confines of the established human law. If you are married and are reluctant to keep your promise and go after your neighbor's wife, well good luck with opening that can!

You see, what you don't know is that your neighbor and his wife have most likely been through many trials to be where they are now. Granted, this isn't always bad, except there is certainly a history behind why they are so happily married or even unhappily for that matter. Above all things though, at some point along their personal journey, they met, eventually fell in love, and decided to make a promise to each other, forsaking all others. That means, from there on, it was going to be the two of them...only! Obviously, this isn't an easy endeavor. Life happens every day, and circumstances happen to get in the way of that huge romantic flame of love that once existed in your neighbor's home. You, my friend, within the context of this commandment, you have a responsibility as a neighbor to respect your neighbor's boundaries.

I am going to bring up a point now that I will probably mention multiple times throughout this book. Each of the Ten Commandments, by design, was written to instruct us on basic human conduct, to protect our personal well-being, as well as to show us how to treat others in a civilized manner. Think about it. By not obsessively desiring your neighbor's wife, you might not be tempted to give in to temptation and break yet another law of which I will talk about more later. Not only that, but you allow the neighbors' journey to continue, as they have chosen it to be without your interruption. Put yourself in the neighbors' shoes. How would you feel if you had invested one, two, five, 10, 25 years into your marriage, just to have a neighbor, oftentimes a friend, swoop on in and try to take over all the hard work? I know there are situations that will be the exceptions to the rule; however, this imperative, as well as all the others, is a one-size-fits-all when it comes to your personal life application. It may not fit every lifestyle or every partnership; nevertheless, these commands can be applied to any individual's life, including yours, no matter where you might come from or what you might have experienced.

At the end of the day, just stay away from the neighbor's wife. Number one, if the neighbor catches you, you will deserve what is coming. Number two, if she is willing to throw everything away that she has worked so hard to build, on you, then she will most likely be ready to do the same to you after something better comes along. Not to mention, you will have to deal with a significant amount of emotional baggage.

The Neighbor's "Anything"

I am convinced that, by now, you are starting to get the point. Covetousness is at the forefront of every other sin related to our interactions and love towards our neighbor, ultimately because desire begins in the mind, and action follows closely behind. It is always prudent to differentiate between your wants and your needs, lest those things you desire and obsess over lead you blindly into a web of lies. Obsession is a trap. It is a bottomless pit that will enslave you beyond relief in some cases.

The command speaks about slavery. It can be argued that slavery has taken on many forms throughout history. In a modern context, there are some who claim that slavery is dead in America. This assertion can certainly be challenged. But, without a doubt, at one point in our nation's history, it was overt and obvious. Unfortunately, in many parts of the world today, slavery is still a part of life. Although the practice of slavery is an ostensibly unjust ideology and severely archaic, the fact remains that the neighbor's slaves belong to the neighbor. The slave does not belong to you. Bought and paid for by the slave owner. Enough said.

As for the ox and donkey, well, the ox and donkey are the beasts of burden, and these are most likely how the neighbor makes a living. I am certain there are probably different levels of ox or donkey, some that are more expensive than others, some that are stronger than others, some that are used and abused, and some that are brand spanking new. It is plain to see that the reference here is talking about the neighbor's tractor or his nice brand-new Chevy work truck. Either way, nobody wants to go out and buy a new tractor, or a new pick-up truck only to have you go on and copy it. How lame is that? Nobody likes a copycat.

And yes, the same goes for the neighbor's anything. I know, I know. The neighbor is really cool and popular and always has the freshest new gear...but obsessing over the neighbor and his possessions is not a very fitting habit for you. The greatest danger here is that it can potentially lead to breaking other rules, which might eventually lead to you getting hurt or even killed. People are quite protective of their stuff and for good reason. They most likely have worked very hard for everything they have only to have someone obsess over it so badly that they eventually try or successfully take it away. Any way you look at it, this will not end well.

One of the greatest things in life is having the ability to live your life to the fullest. Do not covet, so that you may truly be free. Free to create your journey and determine what every aspect of your life is going to look like. Obsession with others and with things will rob you of that. There is no kind of freedom in an obsessive, or covetous, type of living. None whatsoever. Coveting, the unbridled desire for objects we don't have, is the beginning of breaking every other one of the Ten Commandments. It is the proverbial starting line for completing every other sin.

We live in a world that is getting more and more crowded. It is becoming important, now more than ever, for us to foster our individuality and be original. Don't get caught up in what everyone else is doing! That makes life dull and gray. Originality and who you are bring color to life and to everyone's life around you. Stop looking at the neighbor and start looking within you. You are a unique, free, and beautiful creation, and this world needs you to shine! An obsessive, covetous life steals away valuable time in the pursuit of happiness and the fulfilling your own life's journey. Instead of becoming the best that you can be to offer the world everything you might have to offer, you will spend your life trying to be just like someone else. That is not freedom; that, my friends, is slavery. By birthright, from the beginning, we were ALL meant to be free.

IX

¹⁶ "You must not tell lies about your neighbor." NCV

¹⁶ You shall not bear false witness
against your neighbor. NRSV

¹⁶ Thou shalt not bear false witness against thy neighbour. KJV

Exodus 20:16

CHAPTER TWO

THE 9TH COMMANDMENT

Now, for this rule, I am going to have to disclose something. For many years, I read it and even recited it over and over again in my Sabbath school classes. Admittedly, the version I memorized was the King James Version (KJV), which isn't the most child friendly version today, and it is honestly quite a mouthful: "Thou shalt not bear false witness against thy neighbour."

As I just wrote that last sentence, I could hear a thunderous voice in the back of my mind reciting every word as I typed. I think I might have even envisioned some lightning and cracks of thunder. I say this because this commandment actually sounds very ominous when read aloud in old English. Fast forward to modern times, it simply means, "Don't lie about your neighbor."

There is a whole list of reasons why you shouldn't lie about your neighbor. You see, in the last chapter, it was pretty easy to determine who the neighbor was simply because it is talking about the neighbor's house, wife, tractor, and other things. If I close my eyes, I can see all of those things in my head. In fact, if I look out my window, I can see all those with my two eyes. That is my neighbor. It is here that I want to get into a deeper meaning of the word neighbor. Having said all this, I think it is important that we talk about who your neighbor actually is.

Basically, if we take the same concept of neighbor, and possibly even your neighborhood, and apply it to your school, church, community, city, state, country, and even to the world, we can start to see that the term "neighbor" can actually be quite universal. In fact, if we want to get philosophical about it, Jesus Himself regarded everyone as His neighbor, even those who plotted against him and eventually killed him. In other words, He gave them a certain level of respect as fellow human beings. Either way, according to Merriam-Webster.com, the old English root of the word is *that which is nigh or near, and inhabitant from the root gebūr.* Simply stated, a neighbor is anyone who lives near you. Let me pose a question to you. Now more than ever, in an interconnected world with social media linking all peoples from all corners of the earth, who really is your neighbor? I think we can agree on the universality of the word now more than ever, don't you agree?

So, now that we have established a little commonality with regards to who your neighbor is, let's get to the meat of the rule. Don't lie about your neighbor. It seems very straightforward and simple, but I can tell you for certain that this is probably one of the easiest to trip up on, and most of the time, we aren't even aware of it. What about that gossip? Gossip hurts. And you know why it hurts, because most of the time, there are lies thrown into the mix, or often, the entire story is fabricated. Gossip and rumors have ruined many a people and many an opportunity. Lies have led to many broken hearts, broken relationships, and even physical pain and death in some situations.

I can tell you that, at one point in my own life, someone I loved very dearly, a once upon a time best friend of mine told some lies about me. Not only did those lies devastate me, but they sent me into a deep, deep depression and sadness that I cannot put into words. How was it possible that my best friend in the entire world, the person whom I trusted the most, the person who knew everything about me would betray me this way? She knew every dream, every weakness, every heartache I had ever experienced, every trial I had been through, and I could go on and on, and more impacting yet was the fact that she and I had some of the most fun, amazing, and beautiful experiences anyone could ever enjoy together. And yet, after all of that, she betrayed me and began to spread a horde of lies about me.

When you grow up in a broken home, it is difficult to trust anyone in life's journey. So, naturally, after placing my heart into a person's hands that I was sure would never hurt me, only to find out that she would, it drove my soul into the deepest parts of the earth. How could I trust anyone ever again? How could I trust a God, who I was certain had brought us not only into each other's lives but had brought us together to become best friends and eventually lovers, promised to each other, promised to be joined forever.

That is why I turned to the bottle. Something I had promised myself I would never do, mostly because alcohol had ravaged my home as a boy. I eventually gave into my worst enemy and became a slave to its numbing snare. Self-medication is what it is. It was the only way I could get through the days in an attempt to forget the one person with whom I had decided that I was going to live out the rest of my days. After all of that, I realize now, the reason it was so very painful is that I had to let her go softly because, even though she had done me so wrong, in my eyes, she could do no wrong, and I was ready to take her back and continue on life's journey. Somehow, even though I knew it wasn't my fault, I felt I was still to blame. Interesting how that works...

Unfortunately, however, she never came back. In fact, God has kept her out of my life completely ever since I found out that, not only did she take my heart, she had also attempted to ruin me by spreading lies and false rumors. I forgave her, though. I knew that, eventually, the truth would make itself evident. That is one of the advantages of growing up in the school of hard knocks; a person finds out at a really young age that things have a way of figuring themselves out, for better or worse sometimes, every time. Today, I have the honor of being married to my best friend and am happier and more peaceful than I could have ever imagined. The crazy thing is that it only continues to get better as the days go on! How fortunate I am to have lost the other and gained someone better.

Yet, my story pales in comparison to countless others who have been hurt by lies told about them. We hear stories all the time that relate lawsuit after lawsuit citing defamation of character through slanderous and/or libelous attacks. Lying about someone is no joke in the eyes of our society and our modern government. Why would it be all right to do these things without any type of legal and governmental oversight? To think this type of destructive behavior should be allowed in a civilized society without consequence is ludicrous. Slander and libel ruin lives.

Lying ruins personal relationships, professional relationships, business relationships, even relationships that haven't had an opportunity to begin (if you can believe that). That is how far-reaching your little lies can go. You see, lies are the tiny pebbles, the ones that are often overlooked because they can be so very smooth at times. They can even be pretty; they even have a tendency to be well-polished. Nevertheless, a lie dropped into the proverbial pond does indeed have a very, very far-reaching ripple effect. By the time you know it, that tiny little lie has had some major and oftentimes catastrophic repercussions. Consider this; how many countless battles, military operations, and even wars have been waged due to false information? Or worse yet, operations that have been perfectly cloaked beneath false information in order to satisfy a pre-determined agenda? How many conspiracy theories have been proven via scientific facts to have been an actual conspiracy?

Now, I don't want to get out of hand here and just go on and on talking about lies. You may enjoy lying—shoot, it may be the only thing you think you are good at. Fine. But, do you even have any integrity? How does everyone else know you? What are the fruits of your character? How you choose to conduct yourself is ultimately up to you. As I have mentioned throughout this chapter as a warning—the commandment is actually quite specific on how we should not lie about our neighbor. Although it is not advised, you can continue to lie to yourself all you want, but you need to try really hard not to let them pretty little lies get past your teeth. Bad things are sure to follow.

This commandment is clearly a rule that serves in our best interest. "Lying ruins relationships, period." I mean, what good can ever possibly come from lying about your neighbor? I know that, if you do it under oath, it is certainly going to be "no bueno" for you, even if you do it on the down low; are you really that interested in hurting someone else or making their life miserable? From a logical perspective, lies are like spider webs. They start out small and may go unnoticed at first; inevitably, they end up getting out of control. And eventually, the web starts catching pretty things, like innocent butterflies and cute little ladybugs. At the end of the day, not only does Mom or Dad take the broom to the spiders-web, but the spider is most likely going to meet its end, too!

It is actually pretty simple to practice and remember. Simply remind yourself that lying is for devils, and the truth will always set you free; for liars and thieves are one in the same.

VIII

[15] You must not steal. NCV

[15] You shall not steal. NRSV

[15] Thou shalt not steal. KJV

Exodus 20:15

CHAPTER THREE

THE 8ᵀᴴ COMMANDMENT

"**H**ey!" I thunderously barked as I stood in the doorway to my girlfriend's house. It was a beautiful fall evening, and my brother and his girlfriend had come over to visit and have dinner with us. We had just settled down to watch a movie, and almost as soon as I had sat in my chair, I heard what sounded like a muffled banging noise coming from the alley.

The alleyway was very dark, and we were in a rough part of Spokane, Washington. The city had seemingly been overrun lately by a bunch of hoodlums, looking to score a quick buck by breaking into vehicles and stealing not only car stereos, car batteries, purses, backpacks, pretty much anything they could find, but so bold as to go as far as stripping the seals from the doors! Adding insult to injury, not only did a person wake up to a car that had been ravaged but a car that would not start, forcing people to be late or miss a day of work. A violation of privacy, accompanied by the misery of the loss of possessions, loss of work, loss of pay to recuperate the damages, and ultimately a loss of dignity. Unfortunately, for whatever reason, the city at that time was not in a hurry to respond to reported prowlers or theft in a timely fashion. In many cases, it wasn't until hours later. Let me be clear about something. I am the type of person that does not tolerate thieves or stealing. This is the kind of thing that will take me from joy to absolute anger in no time flat.

My ears perked up as I heard a strange noise coming from the direction of the alley. I stood up from my chair and walked over to the door nonchalantly and opened it. As I looked towards my car in the dark alleyway, I noticed something move just beneath the driver's side door. Then I heard it again "thunk." Immediately, I realized that some fool was trying to pry my driver's door window with a metal object, and my first instinct was to bark out very loudly "HEY!" My veins flooded with adrenaline. Without hesitation, I shot out of the house immediately following my report and bolted towards the hooligan at a full-on sprint. Many of you don't know me, but for those of you who do, you know how intimidating it would be to have my 400lb frame sprinting towards you at full speed like a charging bear. I hit the fence and blew it open with sheer momentum on my side. I rounded my car and looked back, only to see my kid brother hot on my heels, scaling my car in a single bound, something straight out of an action movie, like a superhero ready to have his big brother's back. I could feel the gravel under my boots kicking up as I barreled towards the white four-door sedan that sat parked down the alley in the shadows. The would-be thief slipped as he attempted to enter the car at full speed because, after looking over his shoulder, he knew he was about to be caught.

I caught the car as he was frantically trying to start the vehicle and lurched my giant body into the driver's side window. At this point, the young idiot began begging for his life. I began to rain haymaker after haymaker into the dark cabin of his vehicle, while his two accomplices were trying to pull him away from my wrath. When all of a sudden, the overhead light came on, and it was my little brother who had now entered the arena in the front seat of a late model Oldsmobile sedan. I say my "little" brother only because he does not have all the mass that I have, yet very massive still. We have the similar genes, and I can say proudly that my brother is a football playing, rugby killing, state wrestling champion, power-lifting hulk of a human being. It was a very proud moment to be engaged in combat against evil with my brother at that moment. I actually kind of lost my focus on beating some sense into the thieving fool I was dealing with because I noticed that, while my brother was wrestling with the fool in the passenger side, he was also taking care of the fool in the back seat, who was trying to keep my brother from pulling his opponent out of the vehicle.

Another thing I noticed was that homie in the back seat, as well as the fool I was taking care of, were crying. Both of them in full-on tears. Weeping. Fixing my gaze and attention back over at the driver, he was pleading for his life. Begging for us to let them go and repeating, "I am sorry, I am sooory" in between sobs and tears. I felt compassion then and stopped hitting the young man. Once I stopped swinging, he managed to sink down into the floorboard of the sedan and start the vehicle. In his desperation, the crazy fool was going to drive away while lying on the floorboard of the car. "BLACK! LET HIM GO! GET OUT OF THE CAR...JUST LET THEM GO!!!" I commanded my brother. He did. And as soon as I saw that he was out of the car, I pulled my body out of the window. And just as I had foreseen the thief was going to do, he pulled down the shifter and slammed on the accelerator while still lying beneath the dashboard. The door was still open as they sped away, and apparently, my adrenaline-filled brother wanted some more action and chased them down the alley and into the street full speed, ensuring that they wouldn't stop for more. I called him back.

As I turned around, I noticed both of our girlfriends standing in the alley over by our cars. They had been cheering us on as we gave these fools a bit of street justice. By now, the neighbors had also come out of their houses. After hearing the commotion, one of them came out with some kind of big stick and the other with a bat. They asked us if we were alright as we all stood in a circle listening to the sound of the getaway car screeching down the roadway in the distance. We called 911 and reported the incident, and sure enough, we were forwarded to the community policing agency, and it wasn't until the next day that an officer showed up for a statement.

I am not going to get into the argument of whether my actions were right or wrong. I will state, however, that my brother did absolutely nothing wrong because he simply acted on instinct only by the sound of my voice. He was going to protect me, have my back so to speak. True story. He was cuddled with his girlfriend, facing the opposite way of the door, and reacted simply by hearing the tone in my voice by way of jumping over the couch, jumping over the fence onto the hood of my car and over the top in an attempt to have his big brother's back. I will admit that violence is never the answer. Except that it should also be acknowledged that the ghetto plays by a different set of rules.

Nevertheless, this is a great example as to why I consider myself a disciple of Christ and not a Christian. I am a Christian-in-training because I fall short of Jesus on so many levels. I have a tendency to relate more to Moses. Jesus never would have struck the thief as I did that night. Alas, Moses did strike the stubborn Egyptian and the innocent rock, and these actions are easier for me to understand. Jesus warned in Matthew 5:30 that, if your hand causes you to sin, it is better for you to cut it off and get rid of it than to lose your soul to sin. There is nothing complicated or violent about this verse. It simply means that, if your sin is so great that you cannot withstand the part of your body that forces you to fall, then you are better off without it in an eternal context. Fortunately for us, there is no sin too great that we cannot conquer with the help of the Holy Spirit and sincere, constant prayer. The thieves in my story are better off losing their thieving hands than their entire lives to thievery.

The Law of God is quite clear with respect to stealing. Just don't do it! There have been many other laws that have existed throughout the history of mankind that treated thieves in a less than desirable way. I am thinking now of the Babylonian King Hammurabi and his famous code. In his code of laws, he states (Law #22): "If anyone is committing a robbery and is caught, then he shall be put to death" (Wikipedia). That is pretty severe if you ask me. Even I felt compassion after meeting with these thieves who had violated my space three times in the same month. Too bad for them, I had gotten to the point where I had been actively listening and waiting for their return. And I delivered, what I thought to be, their just reward.

You know what? That is exactly what it is. Stealing from someone is an absolute violation. Anyone reading this message knows exactly what I am talking about if you have ever been a victim of a theft or a robbery. When I was a baby, my mom was working at a convenience store in Southern California. She was held up at gunpoint and was robbed while she was on shift and the only person on duty at that time of night. To this very day, she can recount the fear she felt while that gun was held to her head. This type of violation is a violation of the worst kind.

Not only is it a matter of taking what does not belong to you, or a matter of stealing something that someone has worked so hard to earn, it is a total breakdown of one's faith in humanity. Most people are good people. I know, because I know a lot of people, and not just Facebook "friends." I mean, I have traveled many places locally and abroad, and I have met and know many, many people, and I can honestly say that most people have good, considerate, and generous hearts towards their fellow man. Stealing from a good person makes them less likely to be as liberal with their giving nature. It makes them leery of their community and of humanity as a whole. Basically, the actions of those very few selfish thieving individuals have a severe impact on the greater good.

Granted, we can make an argument for fictitious characters, such as Robin Hood, who presumably stole from the rich to give to the poor. That doesn't make stealing morally right. There are some very wealthy people in this world who are very generous with their fortune. You should not steal means you should not steal. Period. It does not matter who you are or what particular social strata you find yourself in. Stealing is wrong.

You know why stealing takes me from zero to an angry hulking hero in no time flat? Because I am a simple man, and I come from very humble beginnings. My family was very poor growing up, yet we were taught to share what little we had and always to be willing to give without expecting anything in return. To this very day, I am a person that would give you the shirt off my back as long as you ask me for it. Shoot, there have been times when I have given my shirt, even when unprovoked, simply because I saw a need. That is why I have no tolerance for stealing. Because when you have very little, and yet you are ever so willing to give it away to see someone else's world become a better place, you better believe that type of generosity is balanced by the same amount of retribution. Yes, I know God will give me vengeance as He has promised in Deuteronomy 32:35 stating, "I will take revenge; I will pay them back. In due time, their feet will slip. Their day of disaster will arrive, and their destiny will overtake them" (NLT). This verse prompts me to strive to become a better man each and every day. One should fear (respect) the vengeance of the Almighty. The streets taught me respect, and we will all have our day of reckoning.

Honesty is always the best policy. I am reminded now that it is important to bring up the burden of secret sins as I close. What about stealing when you are absolutely positive that no one will ever find out or don't even realize it is wrong because "everyone else is doing it"? What about those post-it notes you took from work? You ran out of toilet paper and took a few rolls out of the school's bathrooms. What about the illegally downloaded movies or music library that you have? What about the shirt you borrowed and never gave back? Am I splitting hairs here? Have you been absolutely honest on your taxes? Do you pay your fair share? I bring this up because the issue of taxes is such a loaded question, one that has as many arguments as there are people. What is right? You know what, it is interesting that even Jesus was presented with this type of question, and He simply said that we should do what is required of us. "Well, then," Jesus said, "give to Caesar what belongs to Caesar, and give to God what belongs to God." His reply completely amazed them (Mark 12:17 NLT). Essentially, when in doubt, just follow the rules. This will keep you out of trouble, and when there is more doubt, ask someone that is wiser than you.

The lesson in this law is simple in how it applies to our material world. Some have, and some have not. Whatever the case may be, it is in your best interest to avoid stealing and becoming a thief. Freedom exists in a life lived in contentment and absent of sticky fingers. At the end of the day, if the law doesn't catch you and take your freedom, it might so happen that a modern-day King Hammurabi just might. Either way, better to work hard for what you have and keep it simple. Beware, a thief is a liar's evil twin. Someone is always watching, and just as my grade-school teacher always used to say, "A word to the wise is sufficient." Be wise and be free.

VII

¹⁴"You must not be guilty of adultery." NCV

¹⁴You shall not commit adultery. NRSV

¹⁴Thou shalt not commit adultery. KJV

Exodus 20:14

CHAPTER FOUR

THE 7ᵀᴴ COMMANDMENT

This last week, I have been praying for guidance and direction with respect to this particular law. As providence would have it, one of my good friends just happened to publish a Facebook post today with regards to Matthew 5:32 stating, "But I say that a man who divorces his wife, unless she has been unfaithful, causes her to commit adultery. And anyone who marries a divorced woman also commits adultery" (NLT). From that single verse, and as is often the case in social media, facebookers engaged in expressing their viewpoints on the verse and conversation ensued regarding the various intricacies housed within the vast wisdom in this particular scripture. It became quite the lively discussion.

This brings me to a key point with respect to the Law of God. Most, if not all, verses in the Bible can be dissected and are subject to countless variances of interpretation. The beauty of the Law, nevertheless, is that it is stated in a way that is straightforward and direct, almost as though God foresaw that humans, through our overabundant need to complicate things, would have a difficult time understanding these laws, had He not made them as simple and straightforward as possible and applicable to whatever age in time they were being considered in. The command for us not to commit adultery is as straightforward as it gets. In essence, one is bound to his or her oath and must remain faithful to his or her marriage partner. It really is quite simple. As with the previous commands already examined and those yet to come, let me caution here that "simply" does not mean "easy," nor does it mean without depth.

We have too often attributed the merits of this law to the sexual context housed within. The sexual context only scratches the surface. The reality of the matter is that this law is really about relationships and the deep emotional and intimate connection at the core of the marriage. You see, the way with which you treat your spouse with honor is a direct reflection of the way you honor yourself. And the way that you honor yourself is in direct correlation with the way you honor your Creator. They are all intertwined.

Now, at a risk of delving too much into the topic of sex, it is important for us to understand that sex, within the marital context, is the pinnacle of expression between two individuals and the physical moment of union between two very different souls. That is why sex, in the absence of love, is hollow, shallow, and ultimately meaningless; sex, as with any other drug, only lasts so long before the euphoric feelings dissipate. Sexual experiences within a love-filled marriage, on the other hand, become building blocks or physical mental markers that solidify and validate the creation of the new family unit within these specific, tangible, and memorable moments housed in the vastness of time and space. I want you to understand that this law has more to do with relationships than the actual act of physical love and pleasure.

Who?

I have already mentioned that the act of committing adultery is directly related to husband or wife, specifically the marriage union. You see, before there were two, there was only one.

I have always been a romantic. For years and years, I waited to be married. At a very young age, I found that I was really quite good at writing poetry and soon realized that R&B was my absolute favorite type of music. Long story short, everyone always thought that I would be the first one married out of my group of friends. Everyone including myself, and boy oh boy was I excited for it! I have always wanted, more than anything, to have my own son. It is a dream of mine to have multiple children, a dozen or so, and to raise them alongside my beautiful wife. Needless to say, the prospect of getting married right after receiving my high school diploma was priority *numero uno* as soon as I hit the 18-year-old mark. And of course, being a romantic, I had it all mapped out in my mind. In my manhood, I am ashamed to admit that I had even gone so far as to begin planning my fairytale wedding. Of course, this is probably my first admission of these little facts, but deep underneath my hardened exterior, there was nothing more than a soft and gentle loverboy, with dreams of being the perfect husband.

Alas, in 2012, and at the ripe old age of 31, my dream FINALLY came true. It actually was a fairytale story in the end, but what has made it even more special is that, along the way, I had given up believing in my dream. I actually had begun to believe that I was destined to become a monk—living far up in the Himalayan mountains in solitude pondering the deepest questions of life. One of those being, "How is it possible that I, Manuel, was never able to find my soulmate?" Yes, I really was that pathetic deep in my soul because that which I had wanted most had eluded and, on several occasions, in fact, had been denied me.

Fast forward to today, and I must admit I have the most loving wife, more than I could ask for and more than I could have ever dreamed of. Had I known that it was going to be her, I would have asked to marry her 13 years earlier right there on the spot. However, destiny required that I should wait. Now, she certainly has her own story, and she can probably entertain us with her journey as well, which finally led up to her wedding day, where she would meet me at the altar. Just two individuals, two very different people, from very different places, meeting at that one place in that one moment in time to make a promise to each other forevermore. To have and to hold, to cherish above all others, in sickness and in health until death do us part.

It is this very story that has repeated itself for as long as the world has been occupied by humanity. The desire to love and the desire to be loved. Promised before God and witnessed by a chosen group of life-long companions.

What?

"Again, you have heard that it was said to people long ago, 'Do not break your oath, but fulfill to the Lord the vows you have made'" (Matthew 5:33 NIV). What significance does such an oath have?

God is King. He is Supreme Ruler over the entirety of all there is, all there was and will ever be. I understand this is a lot for our small and narrow human minds to comprehend. The subject of God is too much for any person to grasp because God exists in a realm that is too far out of reach for simple corrupt humans. But, if you can picture a king (although no human king comes close to the sovereignty of Jehovah), you would understand that, when you make a promise to any king, you had better keep that promise. Plain and simple.

Let me put a modern perspective on it. I know that everyone talks a hard game when it comes to their political affiliations. And it seems, no matter how good or bad a president is, because we are humans and everyone is a critic, there is always some way to criticize the current president. Let's talk about President Obama. I know a lot of people who have had nothing to say but bad things about this president. However, I can guarantee you that, if any of these folks had an opportunity to shake the president's hand or take a photo with the President, they would jump at the chance. In the blink of an eye, they would. Now, consider this. What if President Obama invited you to his house, and while you were a guest in his house, he asked you for a favor and made you promise to fulfill it? Maybe he asked you for some of your grandma's delicious cookies that you were raving about at the dinner table. Would you not keep your promise? Why is it important to keep a promise to a President? What if you came again to the President's house because the President fell in love with your charming personality and enjoyed your company, only this time, you swore an oath to protect one of his daughters with your life, for as long as you both shall live; would you not keep such an oath? Would you not keep such a promise to the most powerful man in the world?

Why would you not keep such a promise to the most powerful King in the Universe? What might happen if you default on your promise to the President, and his daughter gets hurt or possibly worse? What do you think would happen then? I can tell you this. The promise made at the altar, whether a religious ceremony or one presided over by law, is a promise made under the authority of the Eternal King and a commitment to guard and protect one of His daughters with your life. For every woman born into this world is born a princess in the likeness of God.

Where?

Where does it all start? It all starts in the heart. You know, the interesting thing about this law and the interesting way in which God has inspired me to write this book's particular order is that this specific law includes the previous three that I have already written about. First, if there is no ring on her (or his) finger, then it is fair game. But, if you begin to fall for your neighbor's wife…well then watch out, because you are guilty of breaking number 10. As I warned in the very first chapter, be careful of lusting after that which does not belong to you, and more importantly, lusting after that which belongs to another because this is where the spider's web begins to be spun.

"But I tell you that anyone who looks at a woman lustfully has already committed adultery with her in his heart" (Matthew 5:28 NIV). I have to confess something. Remember how I admitted a little while ago that I am a romantic at heart, that I am a "loverboy" with a soft cuddly inside? Well, that particular trait of mine is also a severe weakness. I know that every man can admit that lust is a temptation that knows no boundary, and unfortunately, in our modern world, it is emphasized and promoted so much that one can hardly blame another for his shortcomings. This goes for women, too. At a risk of going on a tangent about the dangers of selling sex in our modern era, let me just point out that the adversary knows all too well the weaknesses of mortals, and sex is at the top of the list.

Did you know that Jesus is so bold as to suggest that one should "gouge out his own eye and throw it away" (Matthew 5:29 NIV) if that eye causes you to stumble? That is pretty severe if you ask me. Let us remember that Jesus knows what lives inside each one of our hearts. He also understands that the heart can be a very deceitful thing. Why did Jesus go so hardcore as to suggest you pluck out your eye and throw it away? Because it is better to lose an eye than it is to lose your life eternally. Look, we all have our favorite sins. As creatures of habit, we will always fall back into our same sins for as long as we live. Jesus understood that, which is why he provided an either/or explanation for dealing with sexual sin, specifically adultery. To put it in simple terms, if you cannot control yourself, and if your eyes, or better yet, what you allow your eyes to see is making you a slave to sin, then you should go without eyesight and free yourself from the torment.

Remember when I said that committing adultery is a spiderweb? Well, let's say you decide to glance over rule number 10 and begin flirting with the neighbor's wife. Pretty soon, it is going to become obvious there is something going on. And inevitably, you and the willing neighbor's wife will begin a whole book of lies and spin a web of deceit. Instantaneously, you are caught in the middle of crushing Law 10 and breaking Law 9 simultaneously. Lies, lies, and more lies. From the get-go, the "relationship" has been based on a lie.

It never ceases to amaze me, even within my very own circle of friends, that people caught up in these types of situations don't understand why there is still so much heartache. Something that was supposed to be "fun," an "extra-curricular activity," a break from their present reality turns into all sorts of shenanigans. And for what? What good could possibly come from lying down in a bed of lies?

Remember that I said it all begins in the heart. Well, it also continues there as well. Feelings start to grow, emotions intertwine, souls begin to merge, yet at the end of the day, your entire world becomes a lie. You are setting yourself up for some serious heartache and often irreparable damage. But you carry on. Business as usual, because these lies have distracted you from reality, and soon, you have created an alternate reality, where the neighbor no longer deserves his wife; in fact, in your twisted new universe, he never deserved her in the first place. Lies, all lies.

Then that moment when a lie turns into a robbery: Like a thief in the night, you swoop in and steal your neighbor's wife. It is everything you have imagined it to be. Life is finally perfect. You and she are finally together and making love in a beautiful place and time; however, you find out soon enough that love never existed. It was all part of the same great big beautiful lie. Because guess what? Yes, you may have gotten the girl, and you may get to enjoy her at your leisure, but she is still a married woman. She still has a husband. Now, I know, everything seems to melt away when you are together, the neighbor's wife and you, but the reality is that your neighbor knows there is something going on. He has known it for quite some time now. Oh how we spin our own webs of destruction, how we set our own traps!

When?

Just when did all this adultery/cheating craziness even happen? A tiny seed was planted in your heart almost immediately. From the very first time you set eyes on her, from the very first time you met her as your neighbor, it began to happen. Now that you have decided to water that seed, it has grown into a weed that consumes your very being, from your soul all the way down into your fingertips. Those moments you lay with her in your mind over and over again, up to laying with her physically in the here and now, there never was any difference. It was everything you could have ever imagined and unbelievably so much more.

Now that it is outside your mind, the scandal begins to happen over, and over, and over in reality. Soon, you feel as though you have triumphed over your neighbor, that is, if he hasn't killed you. And quite possibly, the affection and attention she once commanded of you will be sought after by means of another conquest. Yes, dear friend, she will probably get tired of you, too. You were most likely a simple distraction.

Inevitably, you have forgotten what it was like to be innocent, what it was like to have a relationship that does not begin out of scandal. You have forgotten what it is like to start a relationship out of sheer joy without fear of being caught or worse. Soon, you begin to wonder why relationships just don't work for you, and soon, you begin to ask yourself whether it is you that is the problem and the answer, in short, is—Yes! It IS you!

"But when did this happen to me?" you begin to ask yourself.

When did I become this person who has been nothing but an instrument used to break apart a family and so far removed from the goodness by which I was raised? Or if I was not raised with goodness, so far removed from what I always wanted to become? Daily, you sit trapped in your own cage of guilt and held captive by your own wrongdoings.

Why?

Why did you commit adultery? Why did you give into the emotional farce and the sexual temptation? It is simply because you are human. And because you gave into the weakness of the flesh, this action ultimately rendered you a lawbreaker. We can all agree that a person who breaks the law does not deserve to be free. Why did you do it? Sin is like a virus, and if you feed that virus, it will continue to grow without boundaries. By abiding by this law, you can live a life of freedom. I am certain you know of someone, or maybe yourself, who has participated in adultery and knows how enticing and enslaving it actually is. It doesn't take a rocket scientist to understand how it can turn out to be a bad thing. Unfortunately, too many people knowingly, willingly, choose to travel down this path to perdition.

The breaking of this Law has such pain-filled consequences. Most of the time, it does not end well, and the effects of it are so far-reaching. Yes, over time, it seems as though things finally start to settle down and regain some type of normalcy after adultery has ravaged a home. However, years upon years later, the effects are still felt by individuals, especially by the children (if there are any children in the marriage) when infidelity has burrowed itself in the family.

Why did this sin manifest itself inside of you, and why did it get so far? Quite simply, it is because you allowed it to. You lack discipline and self-control. If sexual sin was your *modus operandi* before you were married, you'd better believe it will still be so during and after. It is only through legitimate and deliberate means that one human can stay committed to another human. Without intentional thoughts and actions, a void is created, and in that void is the perfect space for the seeds of covetousness, desire, lust, and adultery to grow.

There are many truths that we are experiencing in a modern world. A significant truth that is hidden in plain sight and is one of the greatest indicators of the moral decline in a civilized society is the prominence of sexual immorality and the utter disregard for the sanctity of marriage. It is written, "Let marriage be held in honor among all, and let the marriage bed be undefiled, for God will judge the sexually immoral and adulterous" (Hebrews 13:4 ESV). In a modern world and within our privileged society, it has come to seem as though long-lasting, faithful, unadulterated marriages have become the exception, rather than the rule. I am not a fool, and I understand that life is complicated, but life has been complicated for every other couple in every other age that has preceded us, so this cannot be an excuse.

It is necessary to point out that, even some U.S. states have laws that delve out significant penalties for those convicted of marital infidelity. Throughout history, it is evident that there are many laws that deal with adultery, and most of them do not end well for the adulterers. In fact, the Bible states in Leviticus 20:10: "If any man commits adultery with the wife of his neighbor, both the adulterer and the adulteress shall surely be put to death" (ESV). Whatever the consequence, laws still remain, and adultery is a steep transgression of the law.

I am hopeful that, at some point, the tides will shift once again, and marriage relationships will go from being disposable to being valued above all else. There are still many cultures today that understand the depth and breadth of the marriage covenant. Even within our own culture, there are some who value longevity and success, rather than immediate satisfaction. It is worthwhile to choose a life free from the entanglements of marital infidelity. Otherwise, the shadows of adultery will follow you for the rest of your life. You should choose to be free, choose to be faithful.

VI

13 You must not murder anyone. NCV

13 You shall not murder. NRSV

13 Thou shalt not kill. KJV

Exodus 20:13

CHAPTER FIVE

THE 6TH COMMANDMENT

Music is such a curious phenomenon; I used to listen to all kinds of music, some of which would undeniably stir something dark that lived inside of me. Some of these songs had lyrics about drive-by shootings, murder, suicide, and other violent and horrible acts. I would jam to countless songs centered on extreme pain, ugliness, and hatred. It didn't matter if it was rap, hip-hop, or rock and roll; certain kinds of music were fuel for my anger and added just the right amount of motivation for my actions or reactions. In fact, in my younger adult years, I had a special CD mix that I would listen to all the way to work, volume turned up, head banging, and hands beating the steering wheel in preparation for my shift as Security at a popular night club. Needless to say, things often got a bit rowdy on the weekends.

In my pre-teen and teen years violent music served a different purpose, it gave me a place to run to. Not the most ideal place, but an escape nonetheless. In hindsight, I now realize that all that this music did for me was to intensify my nightmares related to violence, particularly those of murder and homicide. Oh no! You might be thinking. What is wrong with this guy? Why is he thinking about violence, death, and murder? Well, to be quite honest, that is the culture I grew up in. I am even bold enough to suggest that we, as a society, have gotten to the point where we even glorify violence to an extreme (more on that later). However, where I come from oftentimes it is "kill or be killed," and that is the mentality with which you exist in day-to-day life.

It started back in the days when I was drawn to gang culture. For those of you who have been privileged to be born on the other side of the tracks or just removed from violence whether it is simply because of social status or other reasons, let me tell you that life on the streets is oftentimes worse than any Hollywood movie you have ever watched. It really is survival of the fittest, and it is a world where only the strongest survive. The only reason I am still alive today is that I was removed from my situation and was given refuge in the bosom of an isolated Christian boarding school, in the middle of nowhere USA, and to be completely honest, for the first couple of years, I absolutely hated it.

The idea of being in a gang or belonging to a gang became more than just a calling. As I got older, it seemed as though it was quickly becoming a necessity, and back then, the idea of a one-man army was not the most practical. I am proud to say that, alone I stood, and alone I fought and was feared, but I was about to reach a tipping point. For some reason, I had made a lot of enemies. Music provided the courage to fuel my rage and turn my fears into energy and violent solutions. The idea of "doing what one has to do" was always on my mind. I knew there were individuals who wanted to kill me… therefore, I had to be prepared to kill as well. This is how I lived my pre-teen and early teen years. Sad to say, for many youth today, especially inner-city youth, they are dealing with some of the same if not more exaggerated circumstances. It is true, oftentimes, "in our very own backyards" so to speak! It has gotten to the point where kill or be killed has become a part of urban life, and this neo-urban warfare is only getting worse by the day. It is no longer fight and live to fight another day. It literally is to kill or be killed. There is no other option.

I have my opinion as to what is fueling this breakdown

in common decency and mutual respect. In short, I suggest that American entertainment has ultimately facilitated and encouraged these types of negative behaviors. From Hollywood blockbusters to music, to ultra-graphic video games, there has risen a gross desensitization of our youth and a birth of casual apathy towards murder, random acts of violence, and the loss of human life. Basically, our children have learned that human life has no inherent value. These tragedies, coupled with parents who are becoming more and more disconnected from their roles of actual "parenting," it is no wonder our young people are decaying at such a rapid rate.

With regards to our society, when was the last time you turned on the news and heard that the USA was *not* engaged in some type of conflict, intervention, or strategic maneuvering? It never happens. In fact, the real truth today is that our military engagements are so commonplace now (however necessary they may be, I might add) that we rarely, if ever, hear about them in mainstream media. Now, before I go any further, let me state something very clearly. I AM NOT ANTI-AMERICAN. Actually, I am quite the opposite. In fact, I consider myself to be a patriot and would gladly lay down my life for my country and fellow country men and women. I am proud to be an American. However, as an American, I understand that our role as the current super power requires certain responsibilities that reach much further than our national borders. As the big brother on the playing field, sometimes we need to protect, sometimes we need to assist, and sometimes we flat out need to intervene for the little brothers of the world to get up to bat. Some might argue that we should have no place in this world as the "global police." I can guarantee that most of those arguing that case have not visited the poorest of the poor in other countries, and they have not recognized what a true privilege it is to be an American. There is a clear distinction between duty, as that exemplified by our honorable U.S. service men and women, local law enforcement, and others sworn to protect, versus those acting on behalf of hatred constructs, hate-filled belief practices, and general malice towards others. What I am trying to say here is that there are currently certain groups of individuals who claim their actions are a reflection of patriotism and their love for our country. The objective reality, however, is that their actions only reflect an inner brooding ugliness towards others who are different and quite possibly towards themselves. In many cases, it is obvious that these individuals have inherited their shallow, misinformed, belief systems and, by no fault of their own practice, what they have been taught. In other cases, the veil of patriotism is a veil behind which blatant evil can manifest itself. I digress.

What does everything I just said have to do with the commandment, "Thou shall not murder?" I was always raised to believe that the commandment explicitly stated "Thou shalt not kill," as it is written in the King James Version. However, in my adult life, I have come to the conclusion that to kill and to commit murder are not the same thing. Bear with me if you will. In the eyes of our American law, there are varying degrees of actually killing someone once convicted. There are several options upon which a court might decide, depending on the evidence presented to them and the case set forth by the accusing party. We hear of terms such as "involuntary manslaughter" and "pre-meditated murder" and a myriad of other legal terms, each of which carries with it a particular maximum sentence. So it is true for the Law of God as well. God will actually be judging us accordingly on a case by case basis, individual by individual, and moment by moment. And since He is the most sovereign of rulers, we can guarantee His mercy is infinitely wiser than any other we could ever wish to compare here on earth. His heavenly court system is the gold standard for universal justice.

As a human, I have come to understand that this commandment absolutely and directly warns against and even forbids that malicious act of taking someone's life for selfish and evil motives or personal gain of any sort. I am certain its complexity is much more far-reaching than what I have just stated, but let us be clear that murder, the actual act of committing murder, is a direct transgression of the Law of God. Do you remember the story of Cain and Abel? You know, the story where one brother killed the other brother because the other brother simply obeyed and did what he was told and was praised for it? I am talking about straight-up murder here. The kind that exists when a person is so out of touch with humanity that fellow humans become expendable and worthless: Homicide, assassination, extermination, execution, slaughter, butchery, massacre, genocide...you get the picture. Thou shall not do any of the aforementioned methods of committing murder. It is forbidden.

I have often said the greatest sin you can commit against someone is causing them to sin. Murder is one of those things that will absolutely alter the minds and perceptions of all those involved, especially the victim's family. Tragically, this sometimes happens and is beyond repair. The act of indiscriminately taking human life is easily one of the greatest, if not the greatest, birthplace for vengeance and retribution. How many countless stories have been written, movies made, songs sung, that deal with the pain inflicted by senseless killing and the revenge sought after by loved ones? Making a case for retribution is a story my family knows all too well.

My paternal grandfather was murdered, assassinated in cold blood. It took place in old Mexico on a small hacienda, named *Villachuato*. Living by an old style of life and ruled by an old way of law, it was natural that someday my father would be required to avenge my grandfather's death. Based on that old way of thinking, should my father not fulfill his duty, the responsibility would fall on yours truly to preserve my family's honor. Providence, however, would have a different agenda for my father. My grandmother immediately sent my father away. This happened very soon after the murder of her husband, my grandfather; my father was sent away as an 11-year-old boy. Although hardened by daily hard work, the kind only farmers and ranchers know, he was still just a boy sent into a perilous journey North all alone, on foot, away from the nightmare committed towards my family. Two thousand miles later, and with nothing except the clothes on his back and a small knapsack, my father finally arrived in Tijuana. Now twelve years old, he finally entered the US, where he was given refuge and treatment for a severe illness he had contracted along his journey, which almost took his life. This surely was a story of an epic journey for a boy who was forced to leave his home to preserve his life and the lives of others. But, he was forced to leave everything that was familiar to him, everything he loved, including his mother. Not only did my grandmother lose her husband and the father of her children, she also lost her son. Not only did my father lose his dad, all of us grandchildren lost the opportunity of ever getting to know our *abuelito* (grandpa). So much loss caused by one selfish and evil act.

The fact that my father lost his dad, had to wander on a dangerous journey alone, and had to start all over again from nothing, forced my father to become hard as stone in order to survive. This toughness was an attribute that was forcefully handed down to yours truly. And it was a painful inheritance. So much pain and loss had instantly been handed down through the generations as a direct result of someone's foolish jealousy and their evil actions towards a caring and generous man—my grandfather.

I also never knew my mother's father. No, unfortunately, he murdered himself. Unable to deal with the misfortunes of this world and a hard life with odds stacked against him, he loaded a revolver, put it to his head, and ended his journey. Yes, in my opinion, the completion of suicide is in fact murder. It is still an intended execution towards the self. However, I know in my heart of hearts that God is merciful and will judge each case accordingly, each person mercifully, because life is not easy for anyone, and for some more than others, at times, it is much too difficult to bear. Please do not misinterpret what I am saying here with regards to suicide. Suicide completion or its attempt is full of extreme complexities and an often multifarious series of events. I am not in any way casting any type of judgment; I am simply inciting my grandfather's casualty as a violation of the law as we understand it. In the suicide victim's defense, my human perspective cannot begin to understand fully the events leading up to it or the rationalization at the moment of completion. The ultimate tragedy is the pain that is transferred to those that remain. Grandpa never had the opportunity and privilege of reconciliations, especially to those close to him that he may have severely hurt along the way. I am certain that some wounds still continue to ache.

Certainly, only God knows what is inside the hearts of those He has created. Once again, I believe that heavenly mercy far exceeds human rationale, and I believe that someday I will see my grandfather again; just because the body ceases does not mean that hope does. I am convinced that all those I have lost to suicide will be awarded mercy and judged with heavenly fairness. They will be justly weighed against a measure based on unconditionality, where all things are considered - this is a measure which is a God measure and not a finite human one.

The reason I am sharing short glimpses of my own life is because I know that my family's tragedy does not hold a candle to some of the stories that many of you can tell. For others of you, you may not have ever had to deal with the unfortunate circumstances surrounding senseless killing and the repercussions of this type of heinous behavior. What I can say for certain is that death makes life sad. Murder makes life unbearable.

In a greater context, the command prohibiting murder applies to whole societies as well. A society is simply a reflection of those to which it belongs. Let us remember that Moses was governor over the children of Israel. At the end of the day, when all the dust has finally settled, whether the act was humanly "justified" or not, the taking of human life is something of the most devastating in nature. It causes deep and enduring damage to the soul. It is also very contrary to an ideal world in which death, pain, or sorrow would not exist. Simply stated, the act of one human killing another human is an act of the most inhumane.

That being said, it is important that we talk about war. Every time I turn on the news channel, I hear about some conflict somewhere and the current death toll. People—men, women, teenagers, children, all dead as a result of war. This is where the law becomes a little complicated because, with war, there is inevitable killing and death. I believe the reason God wrote the law with reference to murder was because He did so with the understanding that, on this earth, and while there is still sin and evil that abound on this planet, there will always be war.

Certainly, by now in this project, I hope there is an understanding that the commandment is written to YOU personally. You and only you are responsible for your own actions. All of these Laws were written so that you can carry them close to your heart, so that you might know what a just and moral way to live actually is. The fact, as it remains, is that this particular command illustrates to us how we can be free of a lifetime of bondage by adhering to this one principle rule, "You must not murder anyone" (NCV). By adhering to this simple rule for right living, you can save your soul from endless lifelong torment and possible eternal perdition. And for those who would become victims, they are saved from permanent pain and suffering.

For God has said,

> I will demand blood for life. I will demand the life of
> any animal that kills a person, I will demand the life of

anyone who takes another person's life. "Whoever kills a human being, will be killed by a human being, because God made humans in His own image." (Genesis 9:5,6 NCV)

Speaking of God, what about God? What about a deity who, on one hand, deals in unparalleled compassion, mercy and understanding, and yet, on the other hand, is perceived to be an archaic God who deals in harsh punishment and violence?

For the answer to this deep question, I was impressed that I must reach out to my esteemed colleague and mentor Pastor Ron Sydney. Surely, a laureate of a prestigious Master's degree in Divinity and practicing Christian in the utmost sense of the title would be able to unravel the peculiarities behind an alleged God of war, the Old Testament Lord known as Jehovah.

So, I wrote him an email in which I posed the following question:

"Using the Bible and the Bible alone, can you tell me why the Old Testament God is portrayed as being, in some instances, so violent towards humans? I am not asking about the differences between the Old Testament and New. I am strictly asking about the violence and God's apparent willingness to kill mankind: To murder man. In short, please answer why the Old Testament God is portrayed as a war-mongering, blood thirsty, genocidal, and highly violent deity. Thank you."

His reply was this:

"Based on the specific question you posed to me about this commandment, you wanted me to peruse an obviously challenging question: If God is against killing, why does the Old Testament (OT) portray Him as this tyrant, blood thirsty, insane God, having an inane hunger towards war, blood and death?

"Historically, Christians have had unquestionable difficulties grappling with the realities of the OT God, while at the same time, non-Theists and atheists have capitalized on this 'gift', arguing the goodness of this God, or whether He even exists. In extension of questioning the existence of God, many press continually the idea that the Bible therefore is a total scam and fabrication, written from the shambolic fairytale mind of men.

"One of the main reasons I chuckle at the latter argument of fabrication, is that in this assumption, a great argument for why God DOES exist is revealed; here it is: If man fabricated the Bible, do you really think they would present God as He is presented in the OT? If a god was to be fabricated, most probably the humans who did so would paint this god with all roses and honey, constantly surrounded with harped angels and sweet music. Yet, the God we meet at face value in the OT is presented differently. That this is not a pleasing and dazzling soliloquy of God bends to the fact that God does exist. Since He does exist, and that the clear eternal backdrop of scripture is that 'God is Love', let's now then spend a short time wrestling with why the OT seems to be a canvas of blood and war orchestrated by this God of love.

1. A Perfect God Operating in a Fallen and Sinful World

We have to levy out first in this discussion that God is dealing with a rebellious and fallen world. Sin came in (Gen 3) through the evil manipulation of Satan. Therefore, according to Paul in Romans 5:12,18-19: "Therefore, just as through one man sin entered into the world, and death through sin, and so death spread to all men, because all sinned; [18] So then as through one transgression there resulted condemnation to all men, even so through one act of righteousness there resulted justification of life to all men. [19] For as through the one man's disobedience the many were made sinners, even so through the obedience of the One the many will be made righteous."

2. YVWH

At some point in earth's history, everyone knew about this Jehovah Yahweh God. Seeing that all came from Adam (Gen1,2), it is believed that the knowledge of God's existence was known. There is a question of whether oral tradition became diluted over the years, especially after humanity separated in Genesis 11 at the Tower of Babel. That the knowledge of God could have been lost over the following centuries is more than just possible; it's fact.

3. "God of War" from Jewish Perspectives and Historical Contexts

It is also key to remember and understand that the authors of the "war time God" were all Jewish. This is quite significant, in that whether intentional or not, their writings were 'biasly' bent towards the times and historical moments of the Jewish people. We don't get to see in any details God's work with other nations. This is important to note for me because, whenever we hear about other nations, it was only at pivotal moments, when Israel had interactions with them. In that sense, it would seem that God is suspiciously one sided and favorable of His beloved child Israel. However, there is one story in the OT that gives us amazing access and insight into how God dealt with other nations or people. The entire book of Jonah documents a glimpse of just that. God desired the salvation of the people of Nineveh, a non-Jewish people. What makes this story amazing is, not only was these people enemies of Israel, but also that God tasked an Israelite preacher to preach repentance to them. This for me highlights vividly this point: God desires repentance and relationship over unfavorable judgment. According to the DNA of God's character, He yearns for salvation for ALL people (2 Peter 3:9). With the Ninevites, He hoped to speak through Jonah, offering repentance and salvation to the whole nation. Again, let's be reminded that this is not just some different nation; they were also enemies of Israel. The reason I stress this point is that many have argued that God destroys nations that are against Israel, without warning or opportunity to turn to Him. The Nineveh story tells us the contrary. Yet, without the Hebrew authors educating us on the full stories of the Amorites, Hittites, and the Philistines—to name a few, we don't get to see how God tried everything to reach them as well. Therefore, I believe, when we see God allowing Israel to annihilate these nations, it was indeed His final judgment on them after offering them a way out to repent and turn to Him (Read Jeremiah 46-48).

4. God Relative to the Context of History

It also needs to be understood that war and bloodshed was the way of life at this time in history. Not only in the Bible, but in any historic book that documents some of the bloodiest battles during this era, any respectable scholar and student of history know that this was a very barbaric time. Therefore, God worked within the cultural norms of the time. If Israel were to defeat a nation in battle and leave the majority of that nation alive, that would be unconventional and a bizarre move in the eyes of their enemies. It was customary that, if you wanted a final battle with a nation, you would wipe out the entire nation, including livestock, women, and children. This sounds understandably awful, which it should be. Yet, we are reading this in 2017, as Westerners. We have to be critically honest and respectful to history and historic culture.

5. God Governing within Cultural Norms

Even the way God dealt with His own Israelites seemed harsh to us, but was cultural norm back then as well. When we see God ordering Moses to kill Israelites who disobeyed certain orders and rules of God, these were the civil norms of the time. We sometimes forget that Moses was not only a Prophet of God but a Governor of sorts for the nation of Israel. He had to lead spiritually and civilly. These 'killings' were also done as a form of civil judgments ordered by God.

6. Merciful Genocide

The hardest thing to grapple with is the killing of children. Though we discussed above the historic culture of the time, I believe God in His mercy allowed the killing of everyone, including children. Think on this: if children were left with their widowed mothers, not only would that be a hardship for them (who would take care of them), but also God wanted to wipe away any possibility for vengeance.

7. Judgment

It also needs to be stated that God did not instruct Israel to kill ALL their enemies. Those He did [instruct to annihilate], I believe that judgment time had come for them.

8. Sixth Commandment Emphasis on Murder

HOW this relates finally to the 6th Commandment is simple and clear: all the killing that God did/ordered in the OT was for a purpose of judgment. However, the sixth Commandment speaks to murder in a vindictive, selfish, self-serving, evil way. This makes it different." (email)

God of Wonder, God of Mystery

God is God, and His ways are often mysterious to us. It is only through wisdom and understanding that we can start to grasp some of His most intricate complexities. My colleague and mentor is a seasoned theologian, an exemplary Biblical scholar, and a Master of his craft; yet I am certain that even he is illuminated daily as he seeks to understand the inner workings of God and His absolute nature. We are all mere mortals. Our mortality is certain because death will befall us all. God, on the other hand, is infinite, and so are His ways.

One of my favorite movies of all time is *The Count of Monte Cristo*. In a scene in that movie, Edmond Dantes, the protagonist, has carved an inscription on the stone wall within his jail cell which states, "GOD WILL GIVE ME JUSTICE." I can assure you that this statement is ever so true, for it is written that God has said, "I will take revenge: I will pay them back. In due time, their feet will slip. Their day of disaster will arrive, and their destiny will overtake them" (Deuteronomy 32:35 NLT). So to my father and to my mother, to my family, to my grandmothers, aunties, uncles, cousins, sisters, and brother, to my friends— don't worry. God has promised us justice. To the rest of you who have dealt with the far-reaching pain of homicide, God has promised you justice. For those of you who are guilty of committing murder, confess your sin, repent, and be set free. And for those of you who wish to remain free under the watchful care of the Holy Law, it is simple; let God be your Justice.

I would like to share one final thought in light of all of the senseless killing that has been going on recently in our country. The commandment explicitly says, "Thou shall not kill." Implying that we should not kill so as to preserve invaluable human life, foster human potential, and to minimize the amount of pain and suffering created at the loss of life and loved ones. "Love your neighbors..." He said. And that is what I will do. Be slow to anger and love one another for "Thou shalt not kill" is an invitation to freedom from loss, severe pain, and extreme sorrow.

V

¹² "Honor your father and your mother so
that you will live a long time in the land that
the Lord your God is going to give you." NCV

¹² Honor your father and your mother, so
that your days may be long in the land that
the Lord your God is giving you. NRSV

¹² Honour thy father and thy mother: that thy days may be
long upon the land which the Lord thy God giveth thee. KJV

Exodus 20:12

CHAPTER SIX

THE 5ᵀᴴ COMMANDMENT

I have been contemplating for the past couple of weeks how I was going to approach this commandment. During that time, it has been both awesome and evident that I am exactly where I am supposed to be and doing exactly what I am supposed to be doing at this point in my life. Everything in life has been pointing to it, even the random movie selection from last night for my wife and I to enjoy quoted this very verse, this very command that I am writing about, word for word several times. It is somewhat overwhelming. I am immediately reminded of how humbled I am to have been called to this project. As I look around my workspace here, I notice yet another clue to my existence. A simple sticker from one of the local breweries *No-Li* promoting one of their delectable crafts, named Born & Raised IPA USA. Is it a coincidence? I don't think so.

Born and raised as an American. This is an idea statement that is altogether so complex, so serene, so privileged. The first time I understood the significance of being an American was on a mission trip to Zimbabwe, Africa. Walking through the open marketplace, I remember being approached by locals and literally being asked if they could touch me: "Can I touch you, Please? Can I touch you?" When I asked why, the reply was simply: "Because you are an American...!" Back then, it didn't make as much sense as it does now. I have to admit that now that I am in my thirties, I have a different, deeper appreciation.

I am humbled to have been given such a privilege by destiny and prouder than ever to be an American.

These sentiments and this feeling of national pride are not unique to Americans, though. I am not interested in going on a tangent here, but I want to point out that most people I have encountered in this world are extremely proud of their origins. People seem to be excited by their history, customs, and culture, and everything that pertains to their land, the place they call home. This in my estimation is by no accident. Every tree in the forest, every flower in the field, every bird in the sky, every hair on your head, every child that is born, each by divine appointment, each one placed exactly where it is supposed to be and to fulfill its appointed destiny.

In the end, home is where the heart is, and it doesn't really matter what continent one was born on. Rather, it is the family and community that one is born into where the true value lays. Born and raised as an American is a debt that I owe to my parents, and I now know it is a debt that can never be fully repaid. The sacrifices they made and the trials they endured require their own pedestal and volume. But for now, I can attempt to shed a small light on our familial success and champion great parenting as the key to personal, and societal, victory and progress.

Honor

The very word honor has such an old-world tone to it. A word associated with royalty that demands respect and admiration, regard, and reverence. Honor is a word that seems so misplaced in a modern world. For years and years, the only place I could ever situate the word was when thinking about times when I stood in the courtroom and people referred to the Judge as "your Honor." I often followed suit. In reality, I didn't know exactly what the word really meant. So naturally, I Googled it. (Just kidding, I actually looked it up in a dictionary, before I had any idea what Google was.) The dictionary said this "1. Regard with great respect. Pay public respect to. 2. Fulfill (an obligation) or keep (an agreement). Accept (a bill) or pay (a check) when due" (Merriam-Webster).

What business did a wannabe thug like me have going to the dictionary looking for answers? Honestly, if I had nothing else in this world, I have always wanted at the very least to do right by God in hopes of someday having a better life. I needed to understand what it meant to Honor your father and your mother.

I spoke to my mother yesterday on the telephone. It was Sunday, and it has always been my custom to call her at least once a week. I called Momma to see how things are going and just to "check in." Mom has been the one and only person on the face of the planet that has ever consistently known where I am at any given time. It doesn't matter what city, town, or state I was living in, I always let my mom know my whereabouts just so she would know that I was doing OK. That is just how we roll. My mom and I are the best of homies, not just friends, but homies. I have never felt the need to hide anything from her, and we have always been able to talk about everything.

Mom was easy to get along with. My mother is an angel, and to top it off, she is the best cook on the face of the planet. My "old man" on the other hand, let's just say that he has always been the thorn in my side.

Utter hatred is the best way I can describe the level of our relationship at times. Yes, the very kind that Jesus actually warns about. It is the kind of hatred that breeds outright rage and violent, uncontrollable anger, the kind where all one can see is red, when tunnel vision sets in, honest, temporary insanity and scarier than anything ever portrayed on television. The scenes from various nature shows where two predators are pictured fighting, biting, bleeding, and ravaging each other to death.

That is the kind of hatred we felt towards each other at times. It hurt. It hurt my heart tremendously. How in the world am I supposed to honor such a man?

As the years have progressed and as I have made my own path, I have to confess that I am a changed man. There came a point in my life when I understood that I could no longer hate because it was contrary to who God had made me. I was made to love. Soon after forgiving my old man for his shortcomings, I began to realize the toxicity that had built up and how hatred had consumed me to a fault. Hatred caused me to make decisions and do things that I never would have imagined, had I not been in a fit of rage. The hate that I harbored for one person directly influenced and determined ALL of my other relationships, and it actually began to create a monster inside of me. It got to the point where I began to fear my monster, and I would actually confess to everyone that I only feared two things in this world: God and my own anger. I feared God because I recognized his power and my presumed insignificance, and my anger because it was uncontrollable. I was on a one-way path towards prison or death, no doubt about it.

Like I said, all of that changed once I forgave the unforgivable. Since then, my Father in heaven has opened my eyes and given me an understanding that is beyond this world. Wisdom has been given to me in order that I might understand the great big question of WHY and continue attempting to establish a "normal" life.

Imagine that you were a child, doing what children do. A little boy living on the farm, tending your animals and caring for your family on a daily basis. Your horse is your best friend. All of a sudden, your father, who you looked up to with extreme admiration, is violently and ruthlessly assassinated for no reason other than jealousy. Instantaneously, you are left with the responsibility as the eldest son and most capable, not only to fill your father's shoes and help provide for six siblings but look over your shoulder daily in fear of those cowards attempting to sever the bloodline completely. That is scenario number one. Immediately followed by your mother, with her wisdom, love, care, compassion, and understanding, who does the unthinkable and forces you to leave your home, your siblings and relatives, and your horse, with nothing more than a knapsack on a journey over thousands of miles through most of Mexico. Remember, you are still a little boy, not more than eleven years old, for days on end, night after night alone in the wilderness and vastness of his beloved motherland.

I am going to stop right there. Just to put it into perspective, I want you to think about the trauma you might have endured up to this point if this was your story. Now, think of the trauma that the child must have endured, not to mention the copious amounts of mental fortitude he must have displayed during this series of life-changing events. He went from being a boy to being a man overnight. And within days, became a solo traveler, a refugee in a strange and faraway place trying to make sense of it all. Don't forget his father was murdered, and that was the jump-off point. Are you getting the picture? After years and years of searching, I finally did. In short, I understand that my dad was never taught how to be a father past a certain point, and what he was taught was not ideal to begin with. My dad was never taught how to be a good husband. He had little time to witness it. My dad never knew what it was to have a home. As a result, he never knew how to make us one. All my dad ever knew was how to work, because that is what his father taught him to do, and that is what allowed him to survive. He is the hardest working old man I have ever known in my life, aside from my great-grandfather.

Respect

In the streets, you will find out very quickly what disrespect is. In fact, it doesn't take much at all. Simply wearing the wrong colors or sporting the wrong professional team gear, or even walking down the wrong street can immediately land you in the hurt locker with five or six guys beating you until you stop moving. A simple "bad look" will instantly trigger a flood of insecurity that can result in the instant beckoning of whether you "have a problem?" I know, because I still deal with this at times. Depending on the attacker's mood, it never mattered whether you had a problem; their problems became your beating, just because you looked their way. Disrespect means dissing someone else's hood or set, an action that will undoubtedly get you killed. I know, I have lost many homies this way. Disrespect is simply not acknowledging the presumed hierarchy in the situation. And that is the reason battles continue and the war never ends. Everyone thinks they are supreme 100% of the time. It is a reality that stems from false pride and forced dysfunctional situations and environments.

Honor, on the other hand, means the absolute opposite. Honor is something that is also recognized on the streets. The major difference is that honor is attached to humility. On the streets, it is usually recognized by everyone in the community and labeled as "mad respect." Usually, an honor is bestowed upon an individual who has transcended the polarizing divides and has acted above and beyond for the betterment of everyone in the community.

Honor means acting with respect. Honor means to esteem and admire. Honor (or respect) does not mean love; those are two very different things. I know, because in my home, we were forced to respect (or honor) Dad, and we were all loved unconditionally by my mother. When I look back at what my old man has achieved, through my new eyes of forgiveness, freedom, and maturity, all I can see is an individual who beat all of the odds and gave me life. In a perfect world, the beatings would have been replaced with hugs and the cursing at me with a pat on the back. In reality, my struggle has made me stronger than most, and now I appreciate it so very much. I am a leader in spite of my pain and simultaneously because of my pain. I am a champion because I have received understanding.

I have learned that, in days of old, wealth was often attributed to land ownership. In Mexico, my family owned a small estate. But for my immediate family, and my father's providential flight to the United States, we have had to "start all over again." We started from scratch as a large family in a tiny one-and-a-half-bedroom house. Therefore, when the verse talks about our days being long on the land that my father will give me, I am forced to look further. I am forced to look at the future and not the past. My father, now a proud American citizen, gave me the United States of America. As a result of his gift, I and all of my siblings have access to unparalleled success. His journey freed him from the chains of his old-world responsibility and created a new hope for his future. As a family, we have been given the privilege and honor of being born in and part of the greatest country on earth in the history of the world. The best part about it is this—God has promised me a long life in this land as long as I continue to follow the positive influence and instructions set in place by my parents. Cautioned to remember the valuable lessons they taught me as they raised me into the man I am today.

They weren't alone, however; many people have had a significant role in my development as my current man and the man I aspire to be. God blessed me with individuals who would teach me positive examples and correct ways of going about fatherhood, and the art of being a husband at multiple junctions in my life. They, shall we say, have filled in the gaps and painted a clearer picture for me to follow in my own quest.

Divine Providence has a way of taking the upside down, inside out, torn and tattered and flipping it completely right side up and making it all right and well again. The best part about God is how much a relationship with Him will renew the old and make it all better than it ever was. I had no idea why I was inspired to write this book seemingly from the back to the front. Beginning from the last commandment and moving forward towards the actual beginning. Nevertheless, as I continue to write and as I continue to be open to His guidance, I have finally understood God's motive. You see, how can we understand a holy, just, righteous, and perfect God, when we are mere mortals and sinful beings from the outset? It is impossible to do so: That type of sovereignty and holiness is too far out of reach for us and too distant from our real-world experiences. Yet, God knows that humans understand other humans. With open dialogue and conversation, humans have an uncanny ability to understand each other, to sympathize with one another, to empathize, or to even agree to disagree. Humanity is the true universal language. As I mentioned, we are all in this together. We are married to our human destiny for better or for worse, in sickness and in health until death do us part. Literally.

Here is the message from an all-knowing, all-powerful, and all-present Father. He knows that, by connecting on a human plane and that by us collectively understanding our weaknesses and faults, we can find solutions to cohabitating our blue planet. That is the genius of a perfect Father. He always meets us exactly where we are, at precisely the right moment, regardless of how far we have strayed away from home.

Since I was forced to leave home at such an early age, I made a promise to call my momma to let her know where I was from time to time. Because I ran, boy oh boy, did I run. I ran from city to city and from state to state. By the time I was twelve, I was rarely home. I had discovered that the streets were a more welcome home. Consequently, as I got older, I ran into drugs and alcohol and from woman to woman, all in an attempt to fill a giant void that had existed in my heart since childhood. And all of it to no avail. It wasn't until that day in Hawaii, having broken an ankle and being completely alone on an island with no cell service that I finally gave up. I confessed it all. I gave it all up. I opened up my heart and asked for forgiveness, and I asked God to teach me how to forgive. At the end of it all, I felt a peace in my soul, deep in my heart that I had never felt before. I was finally set free.

Since then, life has been a roller coaster ride, and I still deal with the damage that I caused to myself after so many years of living like a wild child. My old man and I still don't see eye to eye on most things. And my mother is even more of an angel. But you know what? The trials in life only make us stronger people, and roller coasters only get so big. My old man may still be a thorn in my side, but I now love him, because now I appreciate what he tried to do, despite his own circumstances. My mom may still be an angel, yet we just can't seem to get her to stop working so hard. Such is life and so are humans, I suppose. Each of us is unique, and each of us is beautiful, even in our mistakes and in our shortcomings. I am reminded of what my good friend Pastor Ron said in our meeting regarding this book, "Everything (in life) depends on what lenses you choose to see it through."

I choose to look at it this way. The absence of an earthly father at crucial stages in my development forced me to search out and lean on a Heavenly Father. This, in turn, allowed me to notice Godly men during the course of my journey who reflected what I believe God looks like as a father. Consequently, these reflections, in turn, gave me a realistic and tangible human perspective. All of this has allowed me to have an even greater understanding of who God the Father actually is, and now I love Him more, because I appreciate Him more, and I have a feeling this is a phenomenon that is going to continue until the day I leave this earth and continue even beyond that. This is what I believe, and so far, I haven't been wrong. Without a doubt, it is fundamentally a Fibonacci pattern.

You always have the option to choose what you want to believe. I can admit that I tried to live life for a while pretending God didn't exist. Even though it was extremely fun at times, it really wasn't all that it is cracked up to be. "Choose you this day, who you are going to serve. As for me and my house, we will serve the Lord" (Joshua 24:15). It really is a simple choice and one that has to be made daily.

There is one undeniable fact about this commandment that should resonate in your mind. And it is that the command has been written in a way that it is supposed to teach us how to have and develop personal and intimate relationships and all of the intricate components of this feat. The only way that a human can grasp this concept, the concept of relationships, intimacy, and other crucial component of this portion of development, is within the relationship between a child and his or her parents. Here is where foundations are built.

The Ideal Parent and Child

Friends, the commandment to "Honor your father and your mother, so that you will live a long time in the land that the Lord your God is going to give you" (NCV) is simply a way of summarizing how we ought to pattern our lives. Our greatest examples are our parents. I have heard it said that we do not get to choose our parents. And that could not be any truer in my situation, and it cannot be truer in families where parents are far worse or have committed horrific crimes, especially against their own children. For those situations, I am terribly sorry. All I can say is that God will give you justice, my child. I promise.

For the longest time, I didn't understand this verse. You

see, at the root of it, it has nothing to do with love and little to do with respect. It has to do with business. Let me explain. Honoring your parents has to do with valuation. In other words, it deals with the amount of value that you should place on the *efforts* of your parents. Some require less, and some require more. Basically, it goes like this. Love and respect are components of parenting. However, this verse is based on understanding. You have to understand that your parents did the best that they could with what they had and with cards that they had been dealt in their attempt to raise you. It is within this understanding that I am proud to speak about both of my parents, however traumatic my childhood was. At the end of the day, I am stronger for it, and I have been able to reach and comfort many people because of it.

I am not telling you this information so you can be like your parents and do things the same way that they did. I am telling you this to remind you of your opportunity to do better and your potential to be successful! One of the single most important jobs ever devised for a human was raising a child. As I mentioned, an earthly parent should be representative of our Father in heaven. Therefore, you have a responsibility to be the best at it that you can possibly be.

This command is chock-full of ideals. If Mom's dad would have been richer, we might have had better food, better clothing, better education, a better future perhaps. And from a rich family's perspective—if they weren't so busy creating wealth then maybe there might have been more quality time for me. Here is where Divine Inspiration needs to be acknowledged in its wisdom. It is written that you should, "Direct your children onto the right path, and when they are older, they will not leave it" (Proverbs 22:6 NLT). Parenting is an art, and every artist knows that the single most valuable thing one can do to perfect their craft and develop it into all of its uniqueness and potential is to devote lots and lots of time to it.

For you parents out there, be warned that the fifth

commandment is a warning to you and a guide as to how you must conduct yourself in the privilege of parenthood. Ultimately, what it comes down to is this: God is Our Father. Jesus said so Himself, remember? Therefore, you are acting in His stead as you raise one of His precious little children. As my mother has always said, we are not her children; she has borrowed us from God. We are His first. I believe this to be the truest of statements. The Bible testifies this truth by David singing, "You made all of the delicate, inner parts of my body and knit me together in my mother's womb" (Psalm 139:13 NLT) and by God Himself declaring, "I knew you before I formed you in your mother's womb. Before you were born, I set you apart" (Jeremiah 1:5 NLT).

Honor Our Father, with all your heart, soul, mind, and strength and love your neighbor as yourself, so that you will have long, happy, fulfilled and peaceful days upon the land that the Lord your Father will give you. Honoring our Father in heaven is the key component in the quest for true freedom.

PARTE

DIOS

³⁶"Teacher, which command in the
law is the most important?"
³⁷Jesus answered, "<u>Love the Lord your God with all
your heart, all your soul, and all your mind.</u>" ³⁸This
is the first and most important command. NCV

³⁶"Teacher, which commandment in the law is the greatest?"
³⁷ He said to him, "'<u>You shall love the Lord your God with
all your heart, and with all your soul, and with all your
mind.</u>' ³⁸ This is the greatest and first commandment. NRSV

³⁶Master, which is the great commandment in the law?
³⁷ Jesus said unto him, <u>Thou shalt love the Lord thy God with
all thy heart, and with all thy soul, and with all thy mind.</u>
³⁸This is the first and great commandment. KJV

Matthew 22:36, 37-38

PROLOGUE

CONCERNING DIVINITY

What is "divine?" From a human perspective, it is impossible to describe what divinity actually means. We make futile attempts at categorizing various human experiences as divine in hopes of being able to describe the indescribable. For example, the cupcake we just happened to eat was "divine." The fruity beverage that was mixed in such a way as to be "divine" or a trip to a faraway place where one was so taken back by beauty it simply had to be described as "divine." There may be apparitions or moments of sensory overload, either induced synthetically or naturally, which we often have been guilty of describing as "divine." And what about euphoria, as many of us have experienced it, that special place where one feels weightless and absolutely blissful—Divine?

The very concept of *actual* divinity is so far removed from humanity that it is almost impossible to put it into human terms. It may perhaps even be downright sinful to do so. What would one simple human, however complex a biological organism, know about godliness? Certainly, there are some who have thought to achieve that point of transcendence, the pinnacle of self-actualization, and yet each one of these god-men has been met with the same fate, dead and often forgotten. It begs the question then, "Does not true and actual divinity require immortality?" You claim to be a god, except you have failed to continue living your life beyond what is allowed to you by way of your predetermined destiny. To think that *any* human would ever be capable of divinity is certainly a farce. These are things of legends and myths, except that single rare occurrence where the myth can actually be coupled with provable historical facts that continue to unfold and reveal it day by day, year after year.

History has shown us time and time again, human examples of which were elevated to a state of godliness. Mostly a ruling class of individuals, pharaohs, Caesars, Aztec emperors, and many others who personified, or attempted to personify a god incarnate. On one hand, we have to admit that their memory has been preserved throughout history, somewhat qualifying their claim to immortality. Their legacy continues on, and we know and understand some aspects of each of their short existence and accomplishments while yet alive. We must also admit, however, that much of who these people were has died with them and now lies lost in the sand, never to be known again. We are left with a glimpse, and might I add it is often an approved and chosen record of self that has been passed down through the ages. An attempt on their part to be remembered in glorified attributes and absence of faults.

One can argue that all these things can also be attributed to Christ and the "legend" of His actual existence upon the earth. The contrasting evidence between Christ and every other god-man ever recorded in history is that Christ openly and honestly admitted that His intention was never to descend on the earth to rule men and women through fear and manipulation, but rather to set humanity free from their current and future oppressions and oppressors. Christ admitted that His kingdom was not of this earth, stating that, as a Ruler and as a King, He rules a different kingdom, one that likely mirrors His personal attributes. What attributes do we reflect? I heard it once said that follow-ship directly mirrors leadership. This is surely something we humans understand, especially in today's civilized world and in light of our current political contentions. Let me ask you, who is your leader? Who do you actually serve?

It is my personal belief that God, Jehovah God, intends for us to understand that He ultimately rules His kingdom and governs His subordinates under the contexts of unconditional love. Only through grasping the breadth of that simple statement "unconditional love" can we ever have even the slightest chance of understanding the sovereignty of a holy, perfect, and righteous God. The definition of which is contrary to our natural state of being and clouded by an inherited sinful nature. Simply stated, to be divine is to be inhuman. True divinity is transcendence far beyond humanity and beyond all of creation for that matter. To be divine catapults the being into the realm of infinity, and this reality is certainly beyond human grasp or comprehension. Even the greatest of minds exist light years away from this type of understanding.

The law was given to us in written form by means of a divine appendage and written on eternal stone as a safe haven from ourselves, from others who will seek to destroy us, and from time itself. This is an overt testament of the unconditionality of a Sovereign Ruler to His people that, although we have opted for a lesser life, although we have chosen to traverse the globe playing by our own rules and living at times worse than wild beasts, He still offers a place where we can come into rest and assurance, peace, and tranquility. If you shut out all the noise from the world around you, it is easy to see and recognize the value of such an eternal code of conduct.

The most amazing part about it is that, as I have demonstrated in the previous section, the Law of God will constantly and consistently meet you where you are. This statement is no less true of God Himself; He also will meet you where you are every time you make a choice towards Him.

Fundamentally, the law has to do with a Father's love for His children. At its core, it's about unconditional love reciprocated between beneficiaries and Benefactor. Therefore, the law states that as a human you should, "Love the Lord your God with all your heart, all your soul, and all your mind." With all that you are and with all that you have, love the Lord, your Father. It is a simple request of simple beings but an equally large task in a complex and complicated world. As with any relationship, it requires daily attention.

My greatest life project will continue to be the attempt at understanding the inner workings of God Almighty. I am certain of one thing at this point early in my journey; it seems to me that a lifetime will not be long enough. However drawn out my life project proves to be, it is my hope the following chapters will serve to give you a mere glimpse into the Holy of Holies and that it will serve as a starting point in your personal journey into understanding the awesomeness and complexity of the Almighty Father who resides in heaven.

IV

8 "Remember to keep the Sabbath holy. 9 Work and get everything done during six days each week, 10 but the seventh day is a day of rest to honor the Lord your God. On that day no one may do any work: not you, your son or daughter, your male or female slaves, your animals, or the foreigners living in your cities. 11 The reason is that in six days the Lord made everything—the sky, the earth, the sea, and everything in them. On the seventh day he rested. So the Lord blessed the Sabbath day and made it holy." NCV

8 Remember the sabbath day, and keep it holy. 9 Six days you shall labor and do all your work. 10 But the seventh day is a sabbath to the Lord your God; you shall not do any work— you, your son or your daughter, your male or female slave, your livestock, or the alien resident in your towns. 11 For in six days the Lord made heaven and earth, the sea, and all that is in them, but rested the seventh day; therefore the Lord blessed the sabbath day and consecrated it. NRSV

8 Remember the sabbath day, to keep it holy.
9 Six days shalt thou labour, and do all thy work:
10 But the seventh day is the sabbath of the Lord thy God: in it thou shalt not do any work, thou, nor thy son, nor thy daughter, thy manservant, nor thy maidservant, nor thy cattle, nor thy stranger that is within thy gates:
11 For in six days the Lord made heaven and earth, the sea, and all that in them is, and rested the seventh day: wherefore the Lord blessed the sabbath day, and hallowed it. KJV

Exodus 20:8-11

CHAPTER SEVEN

THE 4ᵀᴴ COMMANDMENT

When my wife and I were first getting together, we did the normal things most couples do. We spent a lot of time together, sparsely at first, but as we began to enjoy each other's company, it evolved to the extent that we would eventually spend every available moment with each other. We were simply trying to get to know each other and constantly learning about one another. We exchanged plenty of laughter, as well as some extremely sad and difficult moments; even so, each interaction pulled our hearts closer and closer together. It was the beginning of a relationship, and it was blissful.

My wife was extremely star struck to be with me. I will never forget the look in her eyes as I saw that she started to fall in love with me. The more and more time we spent together, the brighter her beautiful green eyes became and the deeper I could see into her soul. She was hooked. And although I did not want to admit it, she was doing an excellent job of sweeping me off my feet as well. It was new and fresh, awesome, and scary all at the same time. I loved every moment of it then, and I have to confess that I still do.

In her attempt to get to know me better, she offered a suggestion when we were still a young couple. There is a certain book titled *The 5 Love Languages: The Secret to Love that Lasts* by Gary Chapman. I still have yet to read the book, but she convinced me nonetheless to take the quiz to try to determine what my "love language or languages" are. So I did. Reluctantly, I will admit, but I did.

The quiz offered a list for me, and at the very top of that list was Quality Time. As it turns out, the way that I know that someone truly loves me is for them to offer me their undivided attention over a length of time. And let me stress the "*quality*" part of the equation. Now, this, of course, is not the only language I understand. I appreciate and invite every one of the remaining four love languages. I am going to stick to my number one when it comes to this project because, after taking the quiz and discovering for myself what my language is, after some careful analysis and reflection, I found the quiz to be pretty spot on. It was a true revelation! You know, one of those moments in time when all of the dots are finally connected, and all of a sudden, there is that aha! moment. Something I always knew yet had never fully known. Anyways, I am sure you know what I am talking about.

Yes, quality time is what makes me feel validated, loved, important, and cared about. When someone takes a legitimate interest in me as a person, where I've been, what I have been through, who I am, what I am currently doing, and my awesome future, it is easy for me to accept that individual into my heavily guarded inner sanctum. It is at this point and without effort that I naturally pay you in kind. Consequentially, I will become your very best friend, more loyal than any other as long we are playing by the same rules and as long as you do not make the mistake of burning me. Yes, it comes with stipulations; after all, I am only human. And after allowing myself to be used and abused time and time again, let's just say that now there is an extreme amount of caution when trying to figure the other person's agenda. Basically, I wonder, is it me? Or is it because they want something from me? Needless to say, I have become very good at sniffing these things out. In my defense, I think it is wise to have some reservations when it comes to humans. Humans are very selfish creatures.

And some humans will step on anyone or anything to have their way. It is so very sad, yet so very true.

By now you may be asking yourself, what in the world does all of this have to do with remembering the Sabbath day? To be completely honest, it has to do with quality time. It has to do with relationship. The only command written that begins with the word "remember;" remember as opposed to "forget." Obviously, wisdom and foresight knew that we humans would get so busy, so caught up in our own lives and in our own little worlds that it would be easy for us to forget some fundamental things: primarily that we would forget Our Father in heaven.

I am going to be the absolute first to admit to this. I have, at certain points, lived my life completely free. A no holds-barred type of life where I made all of the rules, and they were mine to break. Remember how I spoke about my tumultuous relationship with my old man? Well, as soon as I was able to, I was intent on "teaching him a lesson"—you know, the whole "I will show him" type of attitude. Not realizing that, at the end of the day, I would be the one paying for it. And believe me when I tell you that today, I am still paying for my sins, especially the sins I committed against my body. I wanted to forget the life I had been given, and I wanted a fresh new start where I reigned supreme and there was nothing anyone or anything could do to stop me. I am reminded of an excellent quote from the book, *Ten Commandments Twice Removed* by Danny Shelton and Shelley Quinn where they state, "Rules without relationship result in rebellion!" (118). Now, this could not be any closer to the truth! In my case, I wanted to get away from all of the rules I was forced to obey, and I essentially became a wild child. Living life to the fullest, free and without restraint or limitations, or so I thought.

Unfortunately, at some point, when one lives life this way: godless, with no rules, above the law, and with no regard for anyone other than oneself, something is eventually going to break or give out; it is inevitable. And for me, this happened multiple times. Wake up calls kept a-comin' and I kept a-resistin'. What did it matter? After all, I was young and invincible. Right?

I am sitting here in my mid-thirties, and I often wonder why I made such poor decisions, oftentimes with many tears. I sit here and have to admit that my body is broken. Both of my knees are broken, both of my ankles are worthless—one with a chronic severe sprain, the other I broke in Hawaii. I've broken both wrists, multiple fingers, collarbone, messed up my back I don't know how many times, detached muscles, carved into my body with razor blades, extinguished lit cigarettes on my skin multiple times, jumped out of moving vehicles while fully in the nude (which resulted in the asphalt removing large portions of skin and flesh from my body); there is more, though I am going to stop there. All of these were unfortunate outcomes to me living wild and crazy and ultimately only led to pain, extreme pain in some cases, I might add. All because I wanted to live wild and free with no rules whatsoever. How could I be so foolish, so dumb?

Finally, I am at a positive point in my life. It only took one of the most difficult experiences of my life to begin the process of rehabilitation to get to where I am at now, a place where I am truly and absolutely free. Freedom I found due to a renewed relationship with God, my Father who for some reason, never once left me, no matter how many times I left Him and even cursed His existence. Unconditional, remember?

There are days now when I am certain I can hear my heavenly Father clamoring to me. Passionately, He attempts to remind me of my purpose-filled existence. There are times when I envision the personalized letter that He has written for my journey and tucked safely within my knapsack. A love letter that confidently reads, "Remember Me, remember Who I Am and everything that I have created for you. Remember everything that I have done for you, and remember that I am still working behind the scenes on the things that I am going to give you in the future. Remember me, on My day, week after week, month after month and year after year. Remember Me, because I am always thinking about you, daily, moment by moment—You are my child. Love, Dad (God)."

"Remember the Sabbath day to keep it holy." (Exodus 20:8). What does it mean by holy? Every Sabbath is supposed to be a Holy Day (holiday)! It is supposed to be a day set aside to reconnect with Our Father and family. How crazy is it that we get so worked up about our national holidays, as they roll around once a year, not even realizing that we have been given a *weekly* holiday every month of every year. I am reminded of a verse in the Bible where Jesus said to the politicians of the time, "The Sabbath was made to meet the needs of people, and not people to meet the requirements of the Sabbath" (Mark 2:27 NLT). Just to be clear here, Jesus is NOT talking about the requirements of His Sabbath law; rather He is referencing all of the minor man-made laws the "national leadership" had established. In fact, the only "requirement" in the Law of God is that we not work on the Sabbath. We are to rest on the seventh day. How in the world is that a terrible requirement? Who doesn't like a day off from work?

Here is what it comes down to: Sabbath is first about relationships and second about rest, rejuvenation, and a revival to face the demands of such a challenging world. This is such a critical thing to understand, especially in today's fast-paced, technologically-advanced, modern world.

Technology is changing at such a rapid rate it is now easier to multi-task and successfully carry on and complete multiple projects at once, while raising a family, while remembering to exercise, while remembering to eat right, while being a good citizen and participating in your government and community, while remembering to buy groceries, while forgetting to pay bills, while remembering birthdays, anniversaries, holidays, people's names, pet food, and where you last put your keys! Simply put, in a modern age, Sabbath is a day to DISCONNECT. Now I know that, for some of you, that is simply, seemingly, not an option. You should trust me when I say that disconnecting will ultimately allow you really and truly to RECONNECT with those things that are *really* important and to those things that *really* matter, those things in your physical world, and those in the spiritual realm as well. I hope you understand that the "things" I am referring to are relationships and people.

Do you remember when I mentioned rejuvenation and revival? Well, that is exactly what is happening when you plug your cell phone into the wall. It is recharging! I understand that your cell phone is now an awesome one-stop-shop device for business, play, and pleasure, but even *it* has its limits. Guess what my friend? So do YOU! It is more important that you understand the importance for you to recharge your battery! Quite simply, it is because after you have exhausted your battery, you can't just go to the store and buy a new one. Yup, you get one chance at life, and if you are constantly running, it is going to wear out much faster. Take time to jog, walk, crawl, lie down, and even rest from time to time. When was the last time you went outside, closed your eyes and just were? Listening to the sounds, feeling the warmth of the sun or the cool breeze—*actually being* in the moment? When was the last time you truly disconnected and actually allowed your body to reach 100% before plugging back into society?

You know, we are all children of a God who can actually see the future. He saw well enough ahead and actually created a law requiring us **not** to work. Instead, He wished for us to rest. All by design I might reiterate. And He, God, hoping that in that rest we would **REMEMBER** Him and everything He continually does for our well-being on a weekly basis.

Shelton and Quinn explore the concept like this:

> As we reflect on His infinite love, God restores the joy of our salvation. Particularly as we recall it is God Who is

working in us to make us holy! We remember we are worth nothing less than the price He paid for us, with the precious blood of Jesus. The result is an abiding appreciation of His grace and the love He lavished on us through His Calvary Plan. The object of the Sabbath is "oneness" with God—a day when we wholeheartedly concentrate on our relationship with Him. God wants us to call His holy day a delight, not a day of drudgery (Is 58:13).

In our time-starved world, we can become disjointed from relationships that should be our top priority. The Sabbath is a gift of time- a time for perfect reunion with God and family—a "time out" that restores and sustains our peace and joy.

Didn't Jesus say in the literal Greek translation of Mark 2:27, that He made Sabbath "for the sake of mankind"? This is our God-given holiday from the hassles of everyday life. On this special day, we can ignore worldly demands and enter a time of refreshing from the Lord. God rejuvenates us spiritually and physically.

Our world is sullied by sin—spinning out of control. And our *spiritual vision* becomes blurred from time to time, doesn't it? The Sabbath is God's solution to woo us away from the world and refocus our fragmented attention. For one full day, we set aside individual world interests and we seek our pleasure in Him.

The Lord designed this day to be a memorial of His love, His sovereign power, and our true rest, found in Christ alone. Can you see God's divine plan in this? As we celebrate His goodness, it results in a weekly recommitment to seek first His Kingdom and His righteousness (Mt 6:33) (117)".

Wow! You know, I really like that word "RECOMMITMENT." Recommitment is a vital component to every relationship. Think about it. Every time you show back up to work on Monday morning, you are essentially recommitting yourself to your employer and fellow employees. Every time I have a date night with my wife, I am recommitting myself to her as well. So let me see; what do we have so far: The Sabbath was created for *relationship*, *rest*, and *rejuvenation* for *revival* in our daily repetitions of responsibilities, all within the context of **recommitment**!

Effective and genuine relationships require at a minimum four key components.

1. Connection
2. Communication
3. Care
4. Compassion

The Connection <u>must</u> be intentional. The communication <u>must</u> be open, fair, and balanced. Care <u>must</u> be administered at ALL times. And if you truly care about the persons within the established relationship, you <u>must</u> always attempt to be compassionate of their changing situations. These points are especially relevant in a modern and interconnected world that is evolving daily.

Every quality I have just detailed is a testament to the flawless character of God. As Our Father, He has the perfect harmony of character and strength that make for the perfect father- figure. Our best interests are His best interest, even when we don't understand why things happen the way they do. Unlike humans, God actually is perfect. And our tarnished outlook on life that has been shaped by those humans around us and various events that have taken place in our lives do not apply to a Holy and Righteous and Perfect Father. Be careful not to try to make God fit into a box, friend. Instead, you should remove yourself from your own box or simply think well outside of your closed frame of mind to begin to understand His level of care and compassion.

A relationship with God is absolutely necessary for you to be who you were placed on this earth to become to fulfill whatever destiny is yours, with the *least* amount of pain and suffering along the way. A relationship with God is necessary if you want to be set free from your past, if you want to change your future, and if you want to change the world. And finally, a relationship with God is necessary if you want to be good at any other relationship, period.

My wife is the probably the one person in the world who can qualify that last statement. I have loved her when I have been far from my Father, and I have loved her when I have been near to Him. It is much better, even for myself, when I am close to Him. I am a better man when I am close to the perfect example of a perfect man, husband, and father. And finally, I know what true peace, freedom, and rest actually feel like.

If you want to be the best husband, best father, best employee, best athlete, or best artist, then give God a real opportunity to work in your life. Ladies, the same goes for you! If you want to be the best wife, best mother, best athlete, best artist, best anything in this world, allow God to lead your life. He will make you the BEST version of you. I challenge you to **REMEMBER** the Sabbath day every week, keep it holy, disconnect, and stop working for crying out loud! Work to live; don't live to work, because the good life happens only when you have the freedom to actually enjoy it.

"Be free my child." – God

III

[7] "You must not use the name of the Lord your God thoughtlessly; the Lord will punish anyone who misuses his name." NCV

[7] You shall not make wrongful use of the name of the Lord your God, for the Lord will not acquit anyone who misuses his name. NRSV

[7] Thou shalt not take the name of the Lord thy God in vain; for the Lord will not hold him guiltless that taketh his name in vain. KJV

Exodus 20:7

CHAPTER EIGHT

THE 3RD COMMANDMENT

What is in a name? I am certainly not an expert at names, specifically, the study of names; however, I am going to take the opportunity to impart on you some of my perspective on the subject.

Obviously, names are important. Every human I know has a name or at least is called something. It is true that we usually follow the same tradition and carefully, let me say it again, *carefully*, select a name for our offspring. And no matter what we choose in the end, that name most likely had some kind of significance to us as a family unit, possibly even relevant to a special place, person, or thing of our liking (maybe even a dislike, for that matter). We have a tendency to name things we own. We name our pets, our vehicles, our toys, and other things. Everything about our world is unique with its own identification and with its own identifying name.

Take me for example. My name is Manuel Antonio Pérez. At first glance, there are a few things you can probably gather from my name. First, I have a Hispanic name. You could probably deduce that I am of Latin American descent. What you cannot deduce, however, is that I am of mostly Native descent, indigenous to the continent of the Americas and pronounced by such in most of my physical characteristics, meaning, even though I have a European last name and I happen to speak two European languages fluently, my family and I are comprised mostly of Native American culture and heritage. My father is of the Tarasco Indians of Northern Mexico and my mother of a southwestern US band of Indians, known as the Apache. Interesting to note, before there was a border between the USA and Mexico, these tribes most likely had contact and possibly even traded or were warring nations against each other. But that is all history. The point is, even though I have a Latin-sounding name, if you were to see me, I have mostly been confused with being an ancestor to Native Hawaiians, which I have to admit that I am not. Rather, I am Latino and Native American, and the answer is often, "Oh, but you look like you could totally be Hawaiian." Yes, my friend, it is my indigenous blood and our collective native roots. I am named after my father, as his name is also Manuel. However, I am not Manuel Jr.; that name belongs to my older brother, and it rests with him as it is inscribed on his tombstone.

I have a very smooth sounding name. I am not just saying that. I am told my name is very pleasant, especially when it is properly pronounced in Spanish. Nevertheless, it does not end there for me. I have a whole list of nicknames that I have accumulated over the years. For some reason, one nickname was not enough. It would seem that in all of my travels and in meeting so many different beautiful people, I have acquired many nicknames along the way.

Also, there are versions of Manuel, like Manuelíto, Meñito, and Meño and Manny. The list goes on and on. There are, of course, titles that momma uses to call me and intimate names that my wifey is privy to use as well, but we are not going to go there. The point is that each one of those names and those that are not listed are currently used to identify me to some person on this planet. That person has chosen to remember me by that special name for a particular reason (however unsavory and depending on what chapter in life I was at), and every one of those reasons is special. It means connection, it means relationship, and it means intimacy and memories. All these are experiences that make my human experience so valuable and so great.

I can assure you, for most of those nicknames that I have on that list, there is a name that I have given to that same person who named me. In fact, anyone who knows me knows that most everyone I meet will most likely get a nickname, a pet name if you will. Sometimes, there are unpleasant characters in my life that have received "special" nicknames, but mostly, I assign names for people based on something that stood out to me. Sometimes, it happens right away; sometimes, it takes a little bit of time to pick the right name. Some people I have met have such cool names that I don't have to rename them! Nevertheless, as I mentioned, each name is special, because each name belongs to a person. Or do I dare say that each person belongs to a name? Even my plants have names. Call me weird, but sometimes, I even talk to them. It is a rare occasion that this takes place, but why not? They are alive and making me oxygen, right? They are a part of my circle of life, are they not? Why not acknowledge them and their efforts?

Names are specific to humans. We specifically assign a chosen name for a particular individual to identify them uniquely in the world and to set them apart from everyone else. Granted, there is some obvious overlap here. You know what I am saying. The name chosen for you was special for you. I believe we do this because each one of us is so unique that only a name would be able to store each of us in another's memories properly. Without a name, a face is but a dream. Without a name, does that person even really exist?

From a human perspective, it is easy to contemplate names given to one another and to try to determine whether that name fits that person. This is a game we often play. What about when we are talking about God? Do we have the privilege of also trying to determine whether His names actually fit Him? Is He deserving of special treatment?

What is so special about God that He must command us **NOT** to take His name in vain? He tells us that the misuse of His name is strictly forbidden! Well, once again, this requires us to step out of our comfortable little human world and attempt to comprehend something far beyond our reach. We must first attempt to understand the magnitude of God before we can understand what it means to respect His name.

Now, before I go on attempting to validate the name of the Lord, I need to embellish a little more on a point that I brought up in the previous paragraph, the point about respecting a name and its "meaning." You know, where I come from, and probably the reason I give everyone a nickname, is due to the fact that most people are known by some kind of a tag name. In gang culture, and actually in any group for that matter, most individuals within a tight-knit group will rename each other based on different qualities. Growing up, I can clearly remember there was graffiti all over the place, each set representing his or her own, crossing out a rival set, and always signing their work with their given name. Trigger, Joker, lil' Joker, Matón, La Sad Girl, Creeper, lil' Creeper, Gallo Negro etc., each one of these people proudly represent their set and put their stamp on their territory. This was a huge matter of pride, and it was an action that demands respect.

You must understand that each one of these tags are essentially boundaries. They are "No Trespassing" signs to rivals and law dogs alike. Since most of these gangs are involved in some kind of illegal activity, violence is always the swiftest and most likely course of action if there is ever a looming threat. Like I have said, respect is demanded. I can't tell you how many times, as a youngster walking down the street minding my own business, I was often stopped and asked for my identification, "Hey what do you claim, Ese?" Or, "What set do you belong to? What colors do you identify with?" I can remember there were times when I was scared to death. However, these tough guys, once convinced of my lone wolf story, would often let me be on my way to the library or wherever I was headed. It wasn't until I was older and when I started getting caught up that I really understood the importance of being affiliated with gang culture. I will never forget the day my homie and I were walking across the street. I had never even had an encounter with police, and all of a sudden, the officer said to my friend and I over the loudspeaker, "I am watching you Adrian and Manuel. You better not get into trouble—and stop sagging your baggy pants!" I remember picking up my pants a bit, because yes, they were super baggy, looking over at my friend and asking him, "How does he even know my name?" I have to admit it's kind of scary to get startled by an officer's loudspeaker as you are minding your own business crossing the street! Soon after I found out the officer's name, lo and behold, he was head of the city's gang taskforce squad. He was a good man, and I will never forget him.

Respect is something that is earned and not freely given. I have iterated this point a few times and how it is especially true on the streets. In order to have the slightest respect for the name of the Lord, you must first understand and respect EVERYTHING He has done. That is no easy task. How can we understand the breadth of accomplishments achieved by an immortal, infinite, holy, and perfect God?

To be completely honest, it is a difficult task to undertake. Understanding requires the desire to search and apply factual, relevant data to your reality. But you have to explore. In a modern world, when we have a question, we simply open our nearest web browser and type our question into our favorite search engine and BAM! We are rewarded with oftentimes hundreds, if not thousands, of possible answers. A simple Google search as to the names of God will bring back all sorts of information. The only thing I would remind you of here is beware: not everything on the internet is a true fact (in case you didn't already know that).

When it comes to God, it is important that you weigh your findings against the "Gold Standard" of spiritual and historical documents: The Bible. No, not all Bibles are created equal; that also requires your informed discretion.

If God is a king, and you were invited into His royal court to have a meeting with Him, and let's say it was your first time ever getting to meet God face to face, would you not want to be at your best? How silly would you look if you didn't even know how to address the King? Same thing applies today. How foolish would you look if you didn't pronounce the President's name correctly while in a meeting with him for the first time? How much worse would it be if the president overheard you badmouthing him and his name as you sat in the Oval Office while he was out of the room? That is pretty foolish, if you ask me. Now, think of a God that is always listening; He is always present, and He always knows what is on your heart and in your mind. It is extremely foolish to misuse the name of a being that has that much power in the universe. It is especially foolish for the person that has even a small understanding of the sacrifice God has paid for YOUR eternal life! You can't claim to know God one minute and the next minute start bashing Him behind His back (or so you *think* it is behind His back).

You know what? This is exactly the reason I am so hesitant to call myself a Christian. I believe that Christ is King and that He is God. And if I am supposedly a Christian, someone who embodies the lifestyle of Christ, then I often really miss the mark big time! I am talking to a lot of you "Christians" out there. Some of you are nothing more than POSERS! And that is a very sad thing to be. You neither are, nor are you—just a feather on a pond being tossed around by the wind. By calling yourself a Christian, you are guilty of breaking this commandment. How can you assume the name of a perfect Christ and defile it with your ugly, hypocritical, and blasphemous lifestyle? That is garbage! I am guilty of the same. I have led many people astray;

I admit it. I have led many souls down the road to perdition, and for that, I am forever ashamed. Now, I can only hope God will find them where they are and He will rescue them from the damage I might have caused. For these things I am so sorry. That is why, today, I study and I pray, and I am hesitant even to call myself a disciple. A simple, lowly, student of the Master, because to say that I am at all "Christ-like" is a disgrace.

I have many friends that have been significantly damaged by other so-called Christians, and some of them have yet to recover. I too am one who was burnt very badly by a group of Christians. I went down a long, dark and confused, pain-filled road as a result of how these folks treated me. I would eventually find a nice dark hole where I resided, lost and in ruins. The road back to where I am now was equally painful and extremely difficult. In order to make it back to where I am now, I was required to break completely and allow God to put me back together piece by piece. It is only after being broken and in ruins that I finally understand what it really means to respect and to live fearing the name of Lord. He demands this type of respect because by simply calling on His name from wherever you are in the world at this very moment, you channel a power, His power, which is unmatched anywhere in existence. God is omnipotent, meaning He is "all-powerful," and He is ready and willing to save you from whatever binds you at this very moment and set you free, as long as you are honest and sincere.

The name of God still means more than even your own freedom. It means more than all creation. It means more than everything that ever has and ever will exist in the heavens and on earth. The name of God *is* and *always* will be Lord! The Supreme Ruler over all life and all living things. Yes, it sounds like a super Sci-Fi movie, but even those miss the mark. To be completely honest, in a lot of films, there is often a portrayal of a being claiming to be God Almighty. I can tell you for certain that these portrayals are not only so far from the truth it isn't funny. Truth be told, they are most of the time a blasphemous and a twisted portrayal of the attributes reserved for the character of Jehovah.

How exactly do we know character traits God actually possesses? What exactly is in His name? Well, you know how they say the proof is in the pudding? In this case, the proof is in the inspired Word of God. A simple Google search revealed the following at www.allaboutgod.com:

Names of God: His Titles Revealed in Scripture
"ELOHIM" (or *Elohay*) is the first name for God found in the Bible, and it's used throughout the Old Testament over 2,300 times. *Elohim* comes from the Hebrew root meaning "strength" or "power," and has the unusual characteristic of being plural in form. In Genesis 1:1, we read, "In the beginning *Elohim* created the heaven and the earth." Right from the start, this plural form for the name of God is used to describe the One God, a mystery that is uncovered throughout the rest of the Bible. Throughout scripture, *Elohim* is combined with other words to describe certain characteristics of God. Some examples: *Elohay Kedem* - God of the Beginning: (Deuteronomy 33:27). *Elohay Mishpat-* God Of Justice: (Isaiah 30:18). *Elohay Selichot* - God Of Forgiveness: (Nehemiah 9:17). *Elohay Marom* - God Of Heights: (Micah 6:6). *Elohay Mikarov* - God Who Is Near: (Jeremiah 23:23). *Elohay Mauzi* - God Of My Strength: (Psalm 43:2). *Elohay Tehilati* - God Of My Praise: (Psalm 109:1). *Elohay Yishi* - God Of My Salvation: (Psalm 18:46). *Elohim Kedoshim* - Holy God: (Leviticus 19:2, Joshua 24:19). *Elohim Chaiyim* - Living God: (Jeremiah 10:10). *Elohay Elohim* - God Of Gods: (Deuteronomy 10:17).

"EL" is another name used for God in the Bible, showing up about 200 times in the Old Testament. *El* is the simple form arising from *Elohim*, and is often combined with other words for descriptive emphasis. Some examples: *El HaNe'eman* - The Faithful God: (Deuteronomy 7:9). *El HaGadol* - The Great God: (Deuteronomy 10:17). *El HaKadosh* - The Holy God: (Isaiah 5:16). *El Yisrael* - The God Of Israel: (Psalm 68:35). *El HaShamayim* - The God Of The Heavens: (Psalm 136:26). *El De'ot*- The God Of Knowledge: (1 Samuel 2:3). *El Emet* - The God Of Truth: (Psalm 31:6). *El Yeshuati* - The God Of My Salvation: (Isaiah 12:2). *El Elyon* - The Most High God: (Genesis 14:18). *Immanu El*- God Is With Us: (Isaiah 7:14). *El Olam* - The God Of Eternity (Genesis 21:33). *El Echad* - The One God: (Malachi 2:10). "ELAH" is another name for God, used about 70 times in the Old Testament. Again, when combined with other words, we see different attributes of God. Some examples: *Elah Yerush'lem* - God of Jerusalem: (Ezra 7:19). *Elah Yisrael* - God of Israel: (Ezra 5:1). *Elah Sh'maya* - God of Heaven: (Ezra 7:23). *Elah Sh'maya V'Arah* - God of Heaven and Earth: (Ezra 5:11).

"YHVH" is the Hebrew word that translates as "LORD." Found more often in the Old Testament than any other name for God (approximately 7,000 times), the title is also referred to as the "Tetragrammaton," meaning the "The Four Letters." YHVH comes from the Hebrew verb "to be" and is the special name that God revealed to Moses at the burning bush. "And God said to Moses, 'I AM WHO I AM; and He said, thus you shall say to the sons of Israel, I AM has sent me to you... this is My eternal name, and this is how I am to be recalled for all generations" (Exodus 3:14-15). Therefore, YHVH declares God's absolute being - the source of everything, without beginning and without end. Although some pronounce YHVH as "Jehovah" or "Yahweh," scholars really don't know the proper pronunciation. The Jews stopped pronouncing this name by about 200 A.D., out of fear of breaking the commandment "You shall not take the name of YHVH your God in vain" (Exodus 20:7). (Today's rabbis typically use "Adonai" in place of YHVH.) Here are some examples of YHVH used in scripture: YHVH *Elohim* - LORD God: (Genesis 2:4). YHVH *M'kadesh* - The LORD Who Makes Holy: (Ezekiel 37:28). *YHVH Yireh* - The LORD Who Sees/provides: (Genesis 22:14). YHVH *Nissi* - The LORD My Banner: (Exodus 17:15). YHVH *Shalom* - The LORD Of Peace: (Judges 6:24). YHVH *Tzidkaynu* - The LORD Our Righteousness: (Jeremiah 33:16). YHVH *O'saynu* - The LORD our Maker: (Psalm 95:6).

Names of God: The Lord Revealed in YHVH is the Lord Revealed in Yeshua (Jesus) The LORD who revealed Himself as YHVH in the Old Testament is revealed as Yeshua (Jesus) in the New Testament. Jesus shares the same attributes as YHVH and clearly claims to be YHVH. In John 8:56-59, Jesus presents himself as the "I AM." When challenged by some Jewish leaders regarding His claim of seeing Abraham (who lived some 2000 years earlier), Jesus replied, "Truly, truly, I say to you, before Abraham was born, I AM." Those Jewish leaders understood that Jesus was claiming to be YHVH. This is clearly established when they tried to stone Him to death for what they considered blasphemy under Jewish Law (par. 2-5).

Jesus Today: God Today?

After reading this, there was so much power in the names that I had a literal epiphany! Yes, I did. Here it goes! I honestly believe His command is speaking to those in the **now** as much as it was important to those back **then**. It is becoming even more evident that there are modern-day people who call themselves "Christian," who are nothing more than demons in disguise. I believe that is why God states in the command that He will punish, or not hold those guiltless, those who slander His name. After all, a God knowing all mercy and judging with unconditional love would pardon those who sinned against Him unknowingly.

I encourage you to explore for yourself the depth and the breadth of God's holy name and to accept the challenge of discovering for yourself what a sovereign ruler *actually* looks like. On this earth, and in our lifetimes, we will never understand what it means to be under the authority of a truly just government. Every ruler we will ever have will always miss the mark, because the only way to be absolutely just in every judgment is to have the ability to weigh every aspect of the situation, including *all* the variables that could have altered the outcome. No human is capable of that.

The Law of God transcends all time. So does His holy name. Although this commandment could have been used in the literal interpretation and application to an ancient people, it is still very applicable today in a modern sense. If you call yourself a Christian, the law is speaking directly to you! It is important for you to grasp the extreme honor and privilege that comes with identifying yourself as a Christian and, at the same time, understand the amount of responsibility that comes with claiming you are like Christ.

Jesus said, "I am the way, the truth and the life. No one can come to the Father except through me" (John 14:6 NLT).

Likewise, He states, "Anyone who has seen me has seen the Father!" (John 14:9 NLT). This not only qualifies that Jesus is the Son of God, but that He *is* God—sent down to take on human form: To live among humans. He became human through experience in order that we might connect with a holy and perfect God from our ugly and distant, imperfect humanity for our sake and not His own.

This message is directed to all Christians who have ever been able to justify trampling on a fellow human for your own personal gain or for the advancement of your cause. The Law says very clearly that you will not be acquitted. Be warned!

What exactly is in a name? Identity. Whether you identify yourself to a name or whether you identify yourself by a name, it all comes down to identification. Therefore, any man, woman, or child who finds it necessary to use God's name, or identify themselves with such, should know it is imperative to use it with the utmost respect and honor required of the highest order. Those who have chosen to label themselves after a holy and righteous God should find themselves living up to the prestigious title, striving daily to be holy and righteous examples of such, with simultaneous unmatched humility.

To fear the Lord is to respect His power. It is very simple actually. If you respect the being that holds all the power, then you should also respect His name. And if you don't respect the being, the power, or the names that belong to Him, then be prepared to answer for it. Everyone has a day of reckoning while on this planet. Will you be found chained, tattered, torn, lost and guilty, and most likely having damaged someone else in the process of misusing the name of God? Or will you be found guiltless and free of taking His holy name in vain?

II

⁴"You must not make for yourselves an idol that looks like anything in the sky above or on the earth below or in the water below the land. ⁵You must not worship or serve any idol, because I, the Lord your God, am a jealous God. If you hate me, I will punish your children, and even your grandchildren and great-grandchildren. ⁶But I show kindness to thousands who love me and obey my commands. NCV

⁴You shall not make for yourself an idol, whether in the form of anything that is in heaven above, or that is on the earth beneath, or that is in the water under the earth. ⁵You shall not bow down to them or worship them; for I the Lord your God am a jealous God, punishing children for the iniquity of parents, to the third and the fourth generation of those who reject me,⁶but showing steadfast love to the thousandth generation of those who love me and keep my commandments. NRSV

⁴Thou shalt not make unto thee any graven image, or any likeness of any thing that is in heaven above, or that is in the earth beneath, or that is in the water under the earth. ⁵Thou shalt not bow down thyself to them, nor serve them: for I the Lord thy God am a jealous God, visiting the iniquity of the fathers upon the children unto the third and fourth generation of them that hate me; ⁶And shewing mercy unto thousands of them that love me, and keep my commandments. KJV

Exodus 20:4-6

CHAPTER NINE

THE 2ND COMMANDMENT

The true character of God is one of love. It is an unconditional, steadfast, and enduring type of love. That is who God is and how He wishes to be acknowledged as a Father. But let us remember that we are talking about a deity. We are talking about God, Jehovah God, a being with infinite knowledge and power, not just a simple personification of anything we have ever witnessed within our tangible world. God the Father is a force beyond imagination and, quite possibly, beyond comprehension. This type of power demands respect and admiration.

We need to rewind the hands of time to understand the breadth of this command. Rewind your mind all the way to the creation of all things in existence, including you, me, and our blue planet. This was a time when everything was dark and empty, without any type of real structure. It was a time when the planet was about to receive the gift of life. Imagine with me, if you will.

> God sent His spirit over the planet to ensure that it was ready for what He was about to do. "And God said, 'Let there be light,' and immediately light shown through the darkness and permeated onto the surface of what had previously been dark and desolate. When God saw the light shine through, He smiled and agreed that it was good. Then God decided that there should be a time known as day, and a time known as night. He

separated the light from the darkness through careful arrangements, patterns, and rhythms, and this became the first evening, and the first morning- the very first day of creation.

Next God decided that in order for His master plan to be carried out, He would have to create the next phase in His project. God had to structure an atmosphere that would be the perfect greenhouse for a garden. So, He divided up the ideal proportions of molecules and moisture and created the intimate balance between the water that had already been on the planet to that in the sky. In doing so, He created the ultimate controlled symbiotic environment for all things to exist on earth. A weather pattern that was just right, with just the right amount of precipitation, married to the exact amount of evaporation and the harmonious balance and rhythm of each so that they could continue indefinitely. This was determined to be the second day.

On the third day, the Creator went to work on His garden. He determined the exact place for dirt, for dry land to appear, and He spoke forcing all the water to gather into one place. The continent was formed and it was surrounded by the oceans of water. He stood back and saw that it was perfect. Then He might have said something like, "Inhabitable sphere which I have suspended in the heavens, I want grass in those areas, and I want herbs, and I want fruits, and vegetables, and nuts and every other kind of plant—I want it all to grow forth now and cover the land which I just created." The orb obeyed His command. Grass, herbs and spices, fruit trees and vines, vegetables, nuts, flowers, and plants all grew up out of the earth. It had become a flawless garden escape, and it was a great third day.

Then God wanted the planet to be self-sustaining, He knew that the genetic makeup of all the plants He had created on the previous day would require light and dark, warmth and energy, cycles, and balance in order to function like clockwork. And beyond the earth's atmosphere was another part of heaven what we humans sometimes call space. In this space God created a light for the day and a light for the night, which included the stars as well. And these two celestial beings would play a significant role in the various rhythms of the earth. We call the great daylight Sun and the lesser night light, Moon. The reason being was so that as soon as God removed His presence, the light would not go away, rather these two would provide the necessary energy and light for life to continue on the planet after the Creator had gone away to His next project. Allow me to explain a little deeper. You see, the light that Jehovah emits is enough to sustain all life, but in His absence all things will die. He is, however, a Perfect Designer, and included in His project was every detail. Down to the batteries, if you will, that would sustain life and the life balance and rhythm of everything that we can see, feel, touch, taste, and smell. Astronomic bodies were created to sustain that which would ultimately sustain us. This was the fourth day.

And after the Lord was done with detailing the heavens, He focused his attention once again on the blue planet. In so doing it was on the fifth day that God created more beauty to inhabit the earth. After having already created all of the colors of the garden, flowers, plants, and vegetation, He knew it was time to create fish and whales to fill the vast oceans and freshwater lakes and rivers, as well as the many different species of birds to fill the air and rest in the new trees. And He fashioned these next. And these too were perfect. Now, I want to take a moment here to reflect on something. We are still privileged to see many of these beautiful wonders in our world today. There are fish of every shape, size, and color and birds with every color and song imaginable. It was on this fifth day, in the beginning, God made it so every one of those birds and every one of those fish would continue to reproduce and populate the earth. They too would have a life cycle and pattern in their existence.

The sixth day God created, "the living creature after his kind, cattle and creeping thing, and beast of the earth after his kind: and it was so." (Genesis 1:24 KJV) God spent the day creating every creature that we have ever known on the earth, from the insects to the giant elephants. Each and every one created to inhabit the land brought forth just a few days before. And when He was finished creating every one of these creatures He saw that it was perfect. Yet still, He was not done.

God decides at that very moment that it was time for Him to create His most prized inspiration. A creation that would stand tall and proud above everything that He had previously created. He decided to make us. Humans. He did not decide to create an arbitrary creature, but rather He decided that He was going to craft us in His very image: In the image of God and likeness of other heavenly beings, beautiful and perfect in every way. And God said:

> "They [humans] will reign over the fish in the sea, the birds in the sky, the livestock, all the wild

animals on the earth, and the small animals that scurry along the ground."

²⁷ So God created human beings in his own image. In the image of God he created them; male and female he created them.

²⁸ Then God blessed them and said, "Be fruitful and multiply. Fill the earth and govern it. Reign over the fish in the sea, the birds in the sky, and all the animals that scurry along the ground."

²⁹ Then God said, "Look! I have given you every seed-bearing plant throughout the earth and all the fruit trees for your food. ³⁰ And I have given every green plant as food for all the wild animals, the birds in the sky, and the small animals that scurry along the ground—everything that has life." And that is what happened.

³¹ Then God looked over all he had made, and he saw that it was very good!

And evening passed and morning came, marking the sixth day (Genesis 1:26-31 NLT).

I am going to ask you to take a moment to contemplate everything I just shared with you.

Do you remember when I told you previously that my greatest life work will be to understand the inner workings of God? Well, an attempt to understand God's character is one thing. We have a blueprint for that. But understanding God as Supreme Creator? That is a tall order for an inferior being, even if the human being was designed based on The Divine heavenly schematic.

There is no possible way to understand the enormity of that concept. Have you ever stopped to marvel at the simple design, construction, or mechanics of everything that surrounds you? God, as a Creator, is enormous, and it is too far out there for us to understand. It is much easier to dismiss the creation story as a story because the science behind it all is too complex. Coincidently, it seems that the further and further we march along in earth's history and the more we seem to continue to discover, the easier our inclinations towards disbelief actually become. Should it actually be forcing us to consider that everything in our physical universe was not by coincidence or some kind of cosmic chaos but rather a detailed plan, carried out with detailed planning, by a powerful, designer, engineer, artist, and construction Master? A Master Artisan, who not only engineered the concept, but also created every scientific rule that applies to our particular application? Including every scientific law relative to our earth and universe?

I know it is a lot to believe in, and it is a lot to try to wrap our heads around. I also understand that a great deal of faith is required to believe. However, the evidence for calculated Intelligent Design and Creation is overwhelming. The reality is that, when ALL things great and small in existence are considered, the possibility of a chaotic and accidental explanation for their existence is instantly reduced. Fortunately for us, we are not charged with the task of creating our own universe, heaven, earth, plants and animals, and beings in our likeness. That is not our responsibility. Granted, some have taken these tasks upon themselves as hobbies, such as the attempt to create other humans, which even then is a nothing but a copyright infringement. Others have taken it upon themselves to attempt to reproduce plants or other creatures that *we* have selfishly brought to extinction. And of course, there is the cross-breeding of those living things that already exist. Like I said, there is nothing "original"; it is only simple attempts at forced evolution. The reality is that we humans know we have been created with supreme intellect and ability and that we are simply exercising our God-given rights as the predominant species above all other species on our planet. Whether good or bad, for good or evil, we understand that every other creature, whether plant or animal, is at our mercy. And unfortunately, we have an inherent need to exploit this fact.

That, my friend, is what brings us to the core of this commandment. That is what the foundation of this law is. When we are commanded to avoid creating "graven images" or idols of creatures that fly or creatures that crawl or even celestial astronomic bodies, it is because there are absolute truths that exist here. First, all things were created inferior to humans. The simple fact that humans were the only thing created in the "Likeness of God" and the only creature given "dominion" over everything else is a very significant clue to the ridiculousness of creating an idol of a lesser creation and worshiping it. It makes no logical sense. What can something less significant than you are, whether on an intellectual spectrum or of a physical abilities spectrum, offer you in return for your ultimate worship and admiration? The answer is nothing.

Some may say this only applies to an ancient people, and this command is not nearly as relevant today as it was in old days. People might argue that this type of idolatry is a thing of the past, when people were less civilized, or that, if it is alive today, it exists within pre-modern peoples. Well, I have news for you. Idolatry is still alive today and thriving everywhere; therefore, the commandment is equally as relevant.

God stated in this command, "You must not make for yourself an idol of any kind or an image of anything in the heavens or on the earth or in the sea. 5 You must not bow down to them or worship them, for I, the Lord your God, am a jealous God who will not tolerate your affection for any other gods" (Exodus 20:4 NLT). Clearly, if you cannot grasp how silly it is to worship lesser creations, then you will not grasp the magnitude of foolishness that exists in thinking that any creation is above the God that created it in the first place.

From a theological perspective, these commands were written for the children of Israel after they were delivered from Egypt. History has shown us that Egypt was chock- full of idols and was laden with idolatry. It stands to reason that the "chosen" Israelites had been subjected to and even grown accustomed to certain pagan practices. After 400 years of being in captivity, living and being treated as slaves, I am sure there was a severe breakdown in mental stability on behalf of the enslaved Israelites. Slavery has a way of breaking people down and attempting to erase their roots. I understand how this command was especially relevant to these ancient people. If you will remember, I have already talked about how the Law of God has a transcendent power. It is timeless and is relevant to the past, present, and the future. The second command states this explicitly.

God clearly says that He is a jealous God. Most everyone can understand jealousy. I must admit that I have experienced jealousy many, many times in my life. I have dealt with jealousy so severe at times that I have been forced into an utter rage. The worst of those times have been when it turns out that my jealousy was confirmed because there was a scandal lurking in the midst. Sadly, I know too many of you know what I am talking about. God is constantly dealing with human scandal. Inasmuch, I don't think petty human scandal is the proper scope of His holy jealousy. *Psychology Today* states the following, "Jealousy is a complex emotion that encompasses many different kinds of feelings ranging from fear of abandonment to rage and humiliation" (par. 1). My question to you is this: If this is the best definition for jealousy psychologists can come up with, and they are human like you, how must *God* feel when He has to endure those same feelings or worse? Let me put it this way; if *we* fear abandonment, if *we* are then forced into rage, if *we* are absolutely humiliated because of jealousy, how should God feel? Not only did He create everything in this physical world for our enjoyment, not only did He generate everything in our universe for our sustainability, but He also created *us*. His most prized creation. He did all of this only to have us belittle Him so far as to put some insignificant creature above His majesty? We really are foolish. We can decimate an entire species and bring it to extinction or near to extinction—buffalo, dodo bird, rhinoceros, and countless other species, and yet allow ourselves to adore those very same things that we consider expendable. How should God feel? He has spoiled you, created for you a perfect garden to play in, and you blatantly choose to worship a lesser creation. If we take a step back and look at it from His perspective, we would see that idolatry is downright shameful and utterly disappointing.

One thing is certain. You will receive your just punishment for humiliating God in front of His entire creation. Justly given, because of your affection for other gods, and ultimately, because He is a "God who will *NOT* tolerate your affection for any other gods." He has promised to transcend time with His punishment because an all-knowing God understands human actions, and He understands that foolish parents will teach their children their same foolish hypocrisy:

> I lay the sins of the parents upon their children; the entire family is affected—even children in the third and fourth generations of those who reject me. ⁶ But I lavish unfailing love for a thousand generations on those who love me and obey my commands (Exodus 20:5, 6 NLT).

Why so harsh? Because, in the same way those humans are stewards over the earth and every creation within the earth, so are parents stewards of their offspring. A small child cannot reason to the same capacity and understanding that an experienced adult can. It is wise to suggest that one should carefully weigh what their children will inherit. Will your child unknowingly suffer for your sins? It is always a choice.

Yet, in the same sentence, He promises to "lavish unfailing love" for generation upon generation that hear His voice, guard His word, respect His authority, love Him, and ultimately obey His Law. Where is the freedom in all of this, you might ask? Well, don't worship idols, images of lesser creations, and in the long run, many years after you are dead and gone, your family will still enjoy the blessings of a perfect Father, a jealous Father, I might add, who wants to be loved by you and love you in return. Yes, He is a jealous Father who created humans as supreme above all other creations, whether in the sea, on the earth, in the sky, or in the heavens. A jealous Father created for *you* the *ultimate* playground, and all that He asked was that we be genuine caretakers of our inheritance. That sounds less like a restriction and more like a beneficial condition if you ask me. It sure sounds like a promise for an easier and more enjoyable life. And it certainly does sound like freedom in the grand scheme of things.

No one has ever said that obedience is easy. In reality, being a fool is easy. Nevertheless, both of these paths are a choice. My challenge for you is to understand where you fall on the list of priorities to a Father God. I can assure you are in position *numero uno*. If you are ever in doubt, read the first part of this chapter again, or better yet, grab a Bible and read it straight from the source. That is yet another freedom you can choose to capitalize on or not. True, internal and eternal freedom is always a matter of choice.

I

[3] "You must not have any other gods except me." NCV

[3] You shall have no other gods before me. NRSV

[3] Thou shalt have no other gods before me. KJV

Exodus 20:3

CHAPTER TEN

THE 1ˢᵀ COMMANDMENT

"Fear not, for I am with you," says the Lord (Isaiah 41:10 KJV). I have a confession to make. Just as I sat down to pen this last chapter, the verse that I just described to you is what came to my mind. The reason is that I have been anguished for the last week and a half, trying to figure out how I was going to write this final chapter, how I could effectively end this project. And the path seemed to be ever so elusive. With every other chapter, inspiration would always light my way, and it seemed that wisdom would allow me to hear the words. Here I am, empty and afraid.

How can I do God justice? Who am I that I should attempt to make the case for God and for His sovereign law? Who am I that I should have the privilege of presenting you the King that I serve? I am but a simple man, a willing servant of the Most High. How can I explain the significance of the number one law, the number one rule in the universe, if you have never had an experience with God? I wish that I had the words to describe His awesomeness; I wish that I could relay to you His generosity. I long for some way that I can give you a clue as to the limitless power God holds in His right hand, or the power that He carries in his voice, the strength that He commands with his presence, and the love that drives all of His action. My greatest aspiration would be that I could help guide you into His arms and under His watchful care. If you have come along with me this far on the journey, then hopefully, I have been able to relate to you how simple the answer actually is. God will do all the heavy lifting; all one needs to do is surrender.

"You must not have any other God but me" (NLT). This is not a request; it is a command. Because the moment you replace God or attempt to share His position with something or someone else is the very same moment that you choose to navigate this wretched life solo like a child wandering in the wilderness. You see, friend, no matter how much of an adult you become, you will always be someone's child. And in this same manner, you will always be a child of God first and foremost. This is not an option given to you. There is, however, a choice as to whether one should embrace the fact or reject it.

Over the last nine chapters, we have visited how freedom exists within the confines of obedience of a moral law. I have shared with you how compliance with the Law of God will lessen the burden of life's certain mishaps. I think that, at this point, it is appropriate *ultimately* to address why there is freedom in God as your one and only god. Should you decide to make Jehovah first in your life, you can wake up every morning and go to sleep every night with the reassurance that everything that happened within that very day happened for a reason and according to God's divine will: This is providence. There is absolutely no greater peace on earth than the understanding that every moment in your busy life is being carefully aligned and orchestrated according to a heavenly plan. The kind of peace where joy abounds and tears cease to fall.

When you place God second, third, or dead last in your life, it will never be easy to see how He is working on your behalf. God does not want to be remembered only when you have lost someone. He does not want to be remembered only when you are fired from your job. God does not want to be remembered only on Easter and Christmas. God wants to be number one in your life, and He wants to share in your life, just like any loving family member would.

The thing is this, whether we admit it or not, we all have an inherent need for God in our lives. Some of us skip around and avoid Him at all costs, but at some point or another, the pains of life become too much to handle and too hard to bear. Oftentimes, we inadvertently call on His name as a last resort. Without even thinking about it, we often exclaim, "God, oh God! I need your help!" It is somewhat of a reflex. Is it something you were taught when you were young? Or is it instinct? All animals have instinct. Maybe we instinctively know that we should call on God when we are scared, hurt, confused, or dying. Maybe it is because the very breath that we breathe day in and day out does not belong to us, but rather, it belongs to the Father? And at the back of our minds we know, in our hearts we know, we know that we humans, having the blueprint of God Himself in our genetic makeup, we ultimately long to be with Him.

"I command that you should have NO other gods except for me!" He says. Simply because EVERYTHING is inferior to Him. The examples that I have shared in this book are only a glimpse into the story that comprises what is hidden in the Bible. Time after time, story after story, we see evidence of God and how He always uses every situation to His advantage and for the ultimate sake of humanity. Countless times, He shows mercy to humans, and these are only the ones that are written. The reason the Bible is still around today is because it is still relevant to our times. The same miracles performed in the Bible thousands of years ago are still happening today. We just have a tendency to dismiss them or belittle them down to simple sciences.

God reached down from His mighty throne and, with His finger, began to inscribe on tablets of stone the conditions of His kingdom. His royal rule of law. Written by His finger to signify the fact that He, and He alone, has the power to change any part of the law and written on stone as a symbol to the eternal relevance of His law. Do you know of any human who can carve a permanent inscription on stone with his/her finger? I didn't think so. Because the Law of God is above the laws of man, and it is the basis for peace in any language and across any species in existence. It is the Universal Law of Freedom.

God must be first in your life and in everything you do. When God is first in your personal life, you will have a straighter and surer path towards your destiny. This includes your financial goals, education, friendships, career, family, and of course, your life mate. And once you include God first in every one of these areas and all others relevant to life here on earth, you will notice that life happens easier. Peace is graciously given and received, and life continues much more vibrantly and with less stress. I can tell you for certain that, even those things that we feel like we cannot overcome or have not ever been able to overcome, are possible with the mighty hand of God. How long will you choose to wander without direction? How long will you hold onto your pain?

My fellow Americans, we are a country of hope and inspiration. Our very foundations echo dreams of prosperity and freedom. And for many of us, we have been successful at attaining these things, these fundamental rights. But unfortunately, I know we get caught up. Like spoiled children, we have forgotten where we have come from and what it took us to get here. Then we are reminded, "I am the Lord your God, who rescued you from the land of Egypt, the place of your slavery" (Exodus 20:2 NLT). The very reason this country was established in the first place was because a group of individuals were fleeing religious oppression. They wanted to exercise their inalienable rights to live as free men and to profit from such a dream. However, those days are so long ago and are quickly becoming a distant memory. Now, we feel entitled to the extent that our God-given rights are no longer even related to God, and our Nation under God is now divided. But what would you expect to happen? We have continued to force God out of our schools and homes and out of our government and ultimately out of our own lives. And now, we all live a life of anguish, stress, insecurity, and fear of tomorrow.

America, you have put your faith in the mighty dollar, and now its value shrinks before your eyes. My fellow countrymen and women, you put your time, energy, and effort into work, sex, and football, and now, society is on the brink of collapse. Let me ask you a question if I may.? Where was God when all this was happening? The worship of money gave way to hedonism instead of charity, and the worship of the sins of the flesh have given way to immorality, instead of righteousness and purity of heart. There is a truth about decay. It can be ignored for a while; in fact, it can be ignored for a long while, but it will eventually rear its ugly face, and more often than not, that will happen at the most inopportune of times. Ugly, and often worse than you had first perceived it to be, like rust on a car, a cavity in your teeth, or worst of all—cancer. Trust me, I acknowledge that these examples are non-discriminate. In the same sense, when there is an absolute meltdown in society, it is usually a good indicator that there was an absence of Absolute Sovereignty and the Holy Law that binds that sovereignty to its kingdom of origin.

Jesus Christ is the Prince of Peace and the Lord of Lords. At this point in our earth's history, there is no more denying the fact that Christ actually lived with humans and amongst humans as a human. There is irrefutable evidence to this historical fact. How long then will the skeptics continue to dismiss the story of grace and its relevance within our current and the inevitable eternal contexts? What else is required for you to believe?

You should have no other gods because "He gave His one and only Son, so that everyone who believes in Him will not perish, but have eternal life" (John 3:16 NLT). Can any of those things that currently occupy the bulk of your life and time do this very thing? Can they offer up the life of someone they love in exchange for yours in order that we might ALL live in eternity? There is absolutely no way money can do this. No football team, no job, and no worldly pleasure or possession have this kind of power or even come close to the significance. Here then is a shout-out to the King of Kings, who offered up His own life for your sacrifice.

I am reminded now of our military veterans. I wish I could shake the hand of each one of you for your service, for your bravery and your willingness to lay down your life as the ultimate sacrifice for me, my friends, family, and neighbors—words cannot express my gratitude and admiration. You and your commitment to protecting your people, along with all other law enforcement, fire-fighters, paramedics, and other first responders: The majority of you have manifested on earth the selfless qualities of Christ in our everyday lives. I am certain God has a special place for each one of you. For Christ Himself has said, "There is no greater love than to lay down one's life for one's friends" (John 15:13 NLT).

My prayer is that, as a nation, we invite God back into our country, our government, and ultimately our homes. Our founding fathers understood the importance of God in the proper function of a democracy and republic of the people. They understood that operating outside of the wisdom of God was foolish. They understood, as we do today, that life happens in cyclical patterns and that history will always come around 360 degrees to repeat itself all over again. As a good citizen, you must understand that the Constitution of the United States and the Declaration of Independence are not only documents relevant to our government; they are also warnings against an empire where lawlessness and tyranny rule the world.

"Then if my people who are called by my name will humble themselves and pray and seek my face and turn from their wicked ways, I will hear from heaven and will forgive their sins and restore their land" (2 Chronicles 7:14 NLT). It does not matter who is in office. It does not matter who you elect as your representative. What matters is that God be allowed to administer his council with regards to leading people to greatness. In social, governmental, and personal issues, we are invited by Him, "Come to me, all of you who are weary and carry heavy burdens, and I will give you rest." (Matthew 11:28 NLT). Christ offers peace that passes any kind of human understanding. The kind of peace that instantaneously comes over you, even in the most trying of times and challenging of circumstances; what Christ offers you is freedom, my friend, freedom.

I have been set free. My life story is a book in and of itself. I have done and experienced some ugly and, at times, very horrific things, but I can confess to you now that I am free. Kingdoms of earth rise, kingdoms of earth fall, but the Kingdom of Heaven will stand forever. Today, I know that I belong to His perfect kingdom. And I know that, as long as I am willing to put my faith in God, He will faithfully care for me as my Father. He will provide for me, protect me, guide me, and continue to inspire me. That is what a loving Father does. Remember, a good character, coupled with strength, is what makes an awesome Father! The King of heaven, Jehovah, created these qualities, so I think I am in good company.

> "O Father, Lord of heaven and earth, thank you for hiding these things from those who think themselves wise and clever, and for revealing them to the childlike. Yes, Father, it pleased you to do it this way"; Jesus continues after His prayer by saying "My Father has entrusted everything to me. No one truly knows the Son except the Father, and no one truly knows the Father except the Son and those to whom the Son chooses to reveal Him." (Matthew 11:25-27 NLT).

Call to Action

Before starting today, I was afraid. And I admitted to that in the beginning of this chapter. But I took a step forward and stepped out in faith, hesitantly I might add, after being repeatedly reminded this week that I have the authority of God to speak on His behalf and an obligation to do so. You know, the funny thing is, on my computer screen, I have a Post-It Note that my wife stuck there a couple of years ago as a daily reminder for me. It simply says, "Faith sees best in the dark." The hardest thing you will ever do is allow God to lead your life and have control of every aspect and every bit of drama that inevitably unfolds in it. My friends, always remember there is hope. The more you lean on hope in Him, the easier and more refreshing it actually gets. It is said that it only takes 21 days of repetition to form a new habit. Well, what are you waiting for?

I want to encourage you to put God in and above all else in your life. When God is number one, every other number falls into its intended place. It happens constantly in nature, and rest assured, it will happen in your life as well. Chaos breeds only chaos, whereas the God of all things creates harmony and balance. After all, do you really think it was humans who invented the concept of numbers, mathematics, order, and structure? I invite you to visit the sciences through their Designer's eyes, note their precision, and within them, you will witness God. This is Truth.

If, throughout this book, I have failed to convince you to give God an opportunity and to allow Him to work in your life, I am still at peace knowing that my work was not an exercise in futility. Because ultimately, it is your choice: Herein lies all beauty and complexity of life. On the other hand, I can also guarantee that, if you have read this far, it is because you were challenged to continue turning the pages, and there is something that has inspired hope deep within your soul. I can assure you that it is not me. My partnership with God in this project is the only reason I have come this far, and it is the only reason I will be given the opportunity to share this wisdom with my neighbors. My prayer for you is that you allow yourself the privilege to get to know God in the same way I have, without restrictions and allowing Him access to every part of your journey. This is the truest of freedoms.

William Shakespeare famously wrote, "What is Past is Prologue." History *always* repeats itself. Fortunately, God is patiently waiting! Let go of your repeated failures, and let God give you peace, absolute justice, and eternal freedom. This is my prayer for you.

"Thou shalt have no other gods before me…
For in the beginning…I AM."

EPILOGUE

"**G**ive me liberty or give me death!" These are the immortalized words of Patrick Henry in the year 1775. This line echoes of our humble beginnings as a nation and gives evidence to the tenacity of the human spirit, chasing dreams of freedom and justice in an ever-evolving American lifestyle. "Is life so dear, or peace so sweet, as to be purchased at the price of chains and slavery? Forbid it, Almighty God! I know not what course others may take; but as for me, give me liberty or give me death!" These words continue to shout incessantly in our 21st-century world. Freedom at its core is something that is deserved by all men, women, and children. The ability to act, do, say, and think freely are "inalienable rights" endowed to us by our Creator. And yes, oh yes, all men are absolutely created equal.

Fundamentally speaking, God has allowed us the capacity to choose for ourselves how we might live and carry out our short, yet dynamic, existence here on planet Earth. It is a freedom that is without parallel in nature. No other creation has the same option to the same extreme. Our ability to reason, our cognitive functions, separate us into a category of elite creations, and this is a privilege granted to us because of Divine architecture—from the beginning.

We live in a time of times. Modern age, with its convenience, interconnectedness, hurry, and necessity, forces our lives into an abyss of responsibilities that constantly give way to compromise. Unfortunately, this virulent compromise has made its home in our spiritual lives and religious practices at a rapid rate. Like a cancer, it eats away at the rock-solid foundation that we once housed our lives, our country, our future, our progress, and our eternal consequence upon. Compromise eats at the soul of our nation, our family.

The beauty of modernity is that its complexity fits perfectly into the mold of order established long, long ago on Mt. Sinai and made perpetual by the very finger of the Almighty. Freedom is not something given by man for men; rather, freedom is an idea that should be practiced through obedience to the perfect Moral Law of God. Even those who have never met the goodness and grace of the Almighty Creator understand the universal language of right and wrong, good, and bad. Even they apply it to their daily routines and lives. The question of morality is not comprised then of whether we will die, for that is a given. The question actually begs the answer of how we will choose to live!

Every command written in the Holy and Sovereign Law of God was designed and created for our protection as we inhabit and cohabitate our beautiful planet. Interestingly enough, The Christ had to put the Eternal Law in terms that were easier for us to understand. He simply stated to "Love God First and Foremost, and Love Your Neighbors." He conveniently paraphrased the commands handed to Moses for His chosen people, so that we might investigate their application to our personal lives further. (Most of you who are reading this inadvertently apply the Law of God in your daily lives; others of you might not. I can assure you there was no judgment here.) This book is, in fact, an examination of life within the protection and wisdom of God Himself. Should you at any moment have felt criticized or called out, I am certain it is God's intention to get your attention.

I know for a fact that a world without laws is a world where ONLY the strong survive. The weak are preyed upon, tortured, ruined, and forgotten. Unfortunately, freedom, like anything else, is often taken for granted. It is not until freedom is taken away from the free person that he or she truly begins to understand its value and recognizes their previous fortunes. I can tell you from experience that the moment shackles are placed on your wrists, to then be thrown into the back of a car, transported to a correctional facility, booked, and escorted to your cell, you soon start to realize that freedom is invaluable. After a couple of days of being locked up, it really sets in; after weeks, it becomes almost too much to bear. That moment when you are finally released back into the wild…that is an indescribable feeling. I may not have done a lot of time; however, I did enough. I did enough to know that I will never go back to being caged up like a captive animal, and that is only possible through obedience to the law.

I have many friends who have complained about the constraints placed upon their lives by being "forced" to keep and obey The Commandments. I must admit there have been times in my life when I too have wondered what the real point of having to adhere to such laws is and how it is relevant to my day to day life. Well, that is why I partnered with my Father in Heaven and wrote this book. I wanted to give a seemingly outdated Law and supposed archaic way of thinking the benefit of the doubt and put a positive spin on their perceptions. Instead of thinking of the Ten Commandments as laws that need to be kept and followed to gain entry into the Kingdom of Heaven, why not think of them as everyday practices that actually permit us to live free every day of our mortal lives, which might eventually make the seamless transition into immortality?

Just because the Commandments were written by the God of the universe doesn't mean He is absent from the daily plight of the human being. These rules have existed and will continue to exist well into eternity, unchanged by any human and proven relevant by every temptation we willfully succumb to and by every demon that attempts to undermine their consequence.

Once again, let me reiterate that Jesus Himself was able to summarize the commands into their importance among His modern human counterparts. First, love God with everything you have, for everything He is. Second, love your neighbors in the same way and to the same extremes that you love yourself. Simple, yet so complex. Every command written in the stone tablets stems from the same type of architecture: Each one simple in form and application, yet complex in comprehension, acceptance, and practice. As with so many things in life, I believe that we as humans make the Law of God far too complex. Time and time again, we are shown how the entire Word of God is written in a way that can easily be understood by children. So, if we can set aside our grown-up complications and read the Law of God, understand it, and apply it as a child should, then maybe we can begin to appreciate the inherent value that exists in its overall purpose.

God is our Father. As a Father, as would any decent human father, His instinct is to protect His children from harm and to harbor them from evil. As a Father, He seeks to provide for us a life full of happiness, joy, and oftentimes bliss and euphoria. Our Father wants us to understand the potential of heaven and a life everlasting, so that like children, as His children, we can look forward to being united in the heavenly and perfect ever-after.

The Law provides freedom in our short lifespan here on this beautiful planet. It provides freedom from the harm that our own selfish human desires spawn. It, as with everything else in God's Holy Word, serves as a guide, a compass for good and righteous living. Without this Law, without these Ten Commandments, we would surely fall to the mercy of our selfish desires, end up in ruins, and most certainly meet an untimely death.

The worst thing you can do in life is to make someone else's existence miserable, including God Himself. That is why the penalty for breaking these laws is so severe. Because, in breaking these laws, we ultimately choose to put ourselves above all else, in heaven and on earth, and by doing so, we inevitably sacrifice anyone and anything that gets in our way. In all honesty, if a person is so selfish that they are willing to go to that extent to prove their superiority, then a heavenly community would not be a happy place for them anyways. For in a perfect place, in a perfect moment, all creatures great and small will live together in true and constant harmony and equality: Each species co-existing without want and without need of any kind, in a kingdom of perfection, never-ending happiness and prosperity. All of this made possible by an unchanging, never-ending and perfect God, and the Law He mercifully commands.

No matter what circumstances you may or may not have had in this life to this point, good, bad, or worse, I am here to tell you that everyone has the same opportunity for change, and everyone has the right to live free. All that is needed is a little guidance and a whole lot of prayer.

This book has been an interpretation of the Law of God from my personal perspective. It is an examination of each of the laws and how they are applicable and relevant today, yesterday, and tomorrow. Just as God is, always has been, and forever shall be, so are His codes of heavenly conduct. The Decalogue, along with every word of the Holy Bible, have a transcendent power that supersedes the greatest human minds and the most advanced of modern technologies. It is for these reasons and many more that they certainly should be considered as a fundamental compass for personal development, as well as democratic governmental leadership.

The book consisted of two parts. The first part dealt with the human element of the Law and is designated as **PARTE UNO**. The second part addressed the Laws relating to God's eternal sovereignty and is designated as **PARTE DIOS**. There is a short narrative before each section that leads into the following chapters. The narratives simply set the stage for what I would go on to say in the following pages, kind of like it would be in a stage play or a moving picture. The pre-chapter narratives exist to put the reader in the frame of mind for what follows.

Should you decide to read this book again, may I suggest you do not read this book straight through. Of course, if this is what you decide you should do, that is your choice. I would suggest reading it one chapter at a time with a pause for reflection between each chapter. You should contemplate and meditate on things I have suggested in my writings, and when it is appropriate, you should then continue. This book was written to be a guide: A study of the Law of God and His mysterious and infinite wisdom. Think of it as a guidebook to freedom. As with any guidebook, there is some information that will be relevant to your journey, and there is some that certainly is not.

I am convinced this book is not for everyone. However, since this book has happened to make its way to you, I am confident it was intended to be that way. You may not agree with every point made in every sentence, paragraph, page or chapter, but I can assure you there is something in this book that you needed to read. It is for this reason I am convinced you read it to the end. Ultimately, it was for your sake, not mine. Let me just remind you a final time that, just as each Law stands alone, so does each chapter of this book. Just as each Law works together to create harmony, so does this book attempt to do the same. The difference is that each commandment was carefully written by a divine LORD, and I am just a simple man. The truth is I am a broken vessel with leaks, cracks, and attention issues. So please, my beloved, be gentle.

I began this journey leading with the last of the Ten Commandments. This is the order in which I was inspired to do so. In accordance with an era in which we as humans have become more and more self-absorbed, I am certain it was God's intention, by design, to speak to each of us first by meeting us at our level and within our own self-absorptions. Then, by careful design, we might all take hold of His hand and walk faithfully closer and closer to His throne and towards a clearer understanding of His holy, perfect, and eternal, Absolute Sovereignty.

This book is intended to be a course of study and inner reflection. Although you may or may not relate to some of the examples I have to share, I am certain that, with some calibrated introspection, you might be able to find some fitting examples of your own. *Freedom Triumphant in War and Peace* has been a journey into freedom through obedience of our Creator Father—the "Father who resides in heaven." The previous few pages were merely a roadmap. As previously stated, it is at its best, a simple and humble guide to mortal peace of the highest caliber.

POSTSCRIPT

I was blessed with yet another vision just a couple of weeks following my initial revelation, which is detailed in the preface of this manuscript. I have been privileged enough in my journey to be able to recognize most snakes that actively infiltrate my life. These snakes, be they persons, places or things, which ultimately lead me to sin, are now pretty obvious from my current perspective. However, last night, I was made aware of a particular snake that I may have been overlooking or may have overlooked for a myriad of reasons. The most obvious reason, in my estimation, has been a lack of experience within this environment.

The snake that I was shown to be slithering into my life was not a snake as we would see in physical nature. This snake was actually a three-dimensional "virtual" snake if you will. Yes, it was a digital snake. Its make-up was entirely out of what we might consider being from a digital dimension. It was electric blue, set against a navy blue almost purple backdrop, peppered with lights of various shapes and sizes. It emitted what I can only describe as countless spellbinding electrical pulses across interweaving synapses of multicolored lights. The snake was absolutely beautiful to behold and moved in such a way that it was alluring and hypnotic.

To be continued...

BIBLIOGRAPHY

"Act 2 Scene 1" *The Literature Network*, 14 Aug. 2017, <http://www.online-literature.com/shakespeare/tempest/3/>.

"Honor." *Merriam-Webster.com*. Merriam-Webster, n.d. Web. 14 Aug. 2017.

"Jealousy." *Psychology Today*, Sussex Publishers, 14 Aug. 2017, <www.psychologytoday.com/basics/jealousy>.

"Names of God." All About GOD Ministries, n.d. Web. 14 August 2017. <http://www.allaboutgod.com/names-of-god.htm>.

"Neighbor." *Merriam-Webster.com*. Merriam-Webster, n.d. Web. 14 Aug. 2017.

"Obsession." *Merriam-Webster.com*. Merriam-Webster, n.d. Web. 14 Aug. 2017.

Reynolds, Kevin, director. *The Count of Monte Cristo*. Buena Vista Pictures, 2002

Shelton, Danny, and Shelley J. Quinn. *Ten Commandments Twice Removed*. Remnant Publications, 2014.

Sydney, Ron. "Tho[u] Shall Not Kill." *Tho[u] Shall Not Kill*, 16 Jan. 2017.

Wikipedia contributors. "Hammurabi." *Wikipedia, The Free Encyclopedia*. Wikipedia, The Free Encyclopedia, 5 Aug. 2017. Web. 14 Aug. 2017

"Who Said "Give Me Liberty or Give Me Death"?." YourDictionary, n.d. Web. 14 August 2017. <http://quotes.yourdictionary.com/articles/who-said-give-me-liberty-or-give-me-death.html>.